TRAINING ENGLISCH

Paul Jenkinson

Englisch 9. Klasse

Realschule

STARK

Bildnachweis

Umschlagbild und Illustrationen: Paul Jenkinson

S. 3/168 (Nummernschilder), 6, 8 (Tontopf), 17, 23, 27/178, 28/179 (Gebäude, Broadway, Rodeo Drive), 33, 35, 37, 41, 50, 56 (Foto 2, 3, 4, 5, 6, 8, 9), 60, 61, 63 (Foto 1 bis 6), 74, 77/195, 84, 90/200, 94, 105 (Schild), 107, 134, 139: © Paul Jenkinson

S. 1: © Lee Snider I Dreamstime.com; S. 2: © Ralf Broskvar I Dreamstime.com

S. 3/168: © han Baoluan I Dreamstime.com (Stadt am Fluss); © Josemaria Toscano I Dreamstime.com (Sky City); © Georgios Alexandris I Dreamstime.com (Dorf am Hang)

S. 4/169: © Hannu Viitanen I Dreamstime.com (Farbtube); © Picstudio I Dreamstime.com (Pflanze); © Fibena I Dreamstime.com (Eier)

S. 10: © Jorg Hackemann I Dreamstime.com; S. 11: © Alexander Morozov I Dreamstime.com

S. 15: © Justin Horrocks – www.istockphoto.com (Mädchen); © Tracy Whiteside I Dreamstime.com (Junge)

S. 20: © Yuri Arcurs I Dreamstime.com; S. 26: © trekandshoot I Dreamstime.com

S. 28/179: © trekandshoot I Dreamstime.com (Sunset Bl)

S. 45: © Getty Images (Mark Zuckerberg); © Blomberg I Getty Images (Martin Cooper); http://commons.wikimedia.org/wiki/File:Vaaler_kopi.jpg (Johan Vaaler)

S. 46: http://www.galuba.net/wp-content/uploads/2010/12/facebook-logo.jpg (facebook); © Boumenjapet I Dreamstime.com (Controller); © ab1969 – sxc.hu (Büroklammer); http://klickkomplizen.de/blog/wp-content/uploads/google_logo.jpg (Google); © Garsya I Dreamstime.com (Sicherheitsnadel); © Enrique Gomez I Dreamstime.com (ipod); © Vladimir Grekov I Dreamstime.com (Tacker); © Rasà Messina Francesca I Dreamstime.com (Handy); © Svyatoslav Palenyy – sxc.hu (Laptop)

S. 49: © Galina Zharkova I Dreamstime.com (Mädchen); © Nikolay Okhitin I Dreamstime.com (Autowäsche)

S. 52: © Lincolnrogers I Dreamstime.com

S. 56: © Dean Mitchell I Dreamstime.com (Foto 1); © Jeremy Richards I Dreamstime.com (Foto 7)

S. 63: © Martinmark I Dreamstime.com (Mädchen); S. 70: © Monkey Business Images I Dreamstime.com

S. 72: © Daniele Taurino I Dreamstime.com

S. 78: © Yuri Arcurs I Dreamstime.com (Mädchen 1); © Monkey Business Images I Dreamstime.com (Junge 1 und 2); © Eastwest Imaging I Dreamstime.com (Mädchen 2)

S. 79: © Willeecole I Dreamstime.com (Junge 1); © Monkey Business Images I Dreamstime.com (Junge 2 und 3); © Vadim Kozlovsky I Dreamstime.com (Mädchen)

S. 80: © Lucian Coman I Dreamstime.com; S. 81: © Monkey Business Images I Dreamstime.com

S. 98: © Grand Canyon National Park Museum Collection; S. 105: © NPS Photo (Busse)

S. 109 © Ultrashock I Dreamstime.com (Berglöwe)

S. 112: © Cammeraydave I Dreamstime.com (Laptop); © 2shoes I Dreamstime.com (Mechaniker); © Hannu Viitanen I Dreamstime.com (Vorhang), © Lisa Thornberg – istockphoto.com (Rosen); © Kais Tolmets – istockphoto.com (Gerbera);

S. 116: © Luminis I Dreamstime.com

S. 119: Fotograf: G. Plafker; http://commons.wikimedia.org/wiki/File:LomaPrietaSFMissionStopPlafker.jpg?uselang=de

S. 127: © Franz Pfluegl I Dreamstime.com

S. 132: © Elena Elisseeva I Dreamstime.com (Mädchen 1); © Monkey Business Images I Dreamstime.com (Mann); © Andres Rodriguez I Dreamstime.com (älterer Mann); © Lev Olkha I Dreamstime.com (Mädchen 2)

S. 133: © Paul Simcock I Dreamstime.com (Mädchen 1); © Justin Horrocks – www.istockphoto.com (Mädchen 2); © Chris Mansfield I Dreamstime.com (Polizist); © Carl Durocher I Dreamstime.com (Junge)

S. 140: © Elena Milevska I Dreamstime.com

S. 141 © Nina Fabriano I Dreamstime.com

S. 167: © Olga Sapegina I Dreamstime.com

alle weiteren Bilder © Redaktion

ISBN 978-3-86668-516-1

Inhalt

Autor und Illustrator: Paul Jenkinson

Vorwort

Liebe Schülerin, lieber Schüler,

ist es dein Ziel, in Englisch besser oder sicherer zu werden? Dieses Buch hilft dir, den **Stoff der 9. Klasse** zu **verstehen**, **Grundwissen** zu **wiederholen** und anhand von abwechslungsreichen Texten und Aufgaben intensiv zu **üben**.

- Jedes *Topic* beginnt mit einem **Text** und vielfältigen Aufgaben, mit denen du das **Leseverstehen** trainieren kannst. Die Texte können z.B. eine Geschichte, ein Chat, Werbeanzeigen oder Steckbriefe sein.
- In jedem *Topic* wird ein bestimmter **Grammatikbereich** behandelt. Manche Regeln sind dir ganz neu; du wirst sie im Lauf der 9. Klasse im Unterricht kennenlernen. Andere zentrale Themen kennst du bereits aus den vergangenen Schuljahren; diese Regeln werden manchmal durch neue Aspekte ergänzt. Die Grammatikregeln kannst du dann gleich in **vielen Übungen** anwenden und dadurch **sicherer im Gebrauch des Englischen** werden. Wenn du ein bestimmtes Grammatikthema noch nicht gelernt hast, kannst du diesen Teil einfach überspringen. Die Aufgaben zum Leseverstehen, Wortschatz und Schreiben in diesem *Topic* kannst du in der Regel trotzdem bearbeiten.
- Auch deinen **Wortschatz** kannst du mit diesem Buch erweitern. Im Bereich „*Vocabulary*" trainierst du z. B., Wörter aus dem Kontext zu erschließen, du erarbeitest Wortfelder, beschäftigst dich mit britischem und amerikanischem Englisch und verschiedenen Wortbildungsverfahren.
- Im Bereich „*Using your English*" findest du viele abwechslungsreiche Aufgaben zum **Schreiben**. Die Übungen reichen vom Verfassen einzelner Sätze bis hin zu längeren zusammenhängenden Texten. Hier schreibst du z.B. eine E-Mail oder SMS, füllst ein Formular aus und beschreibst Fotos.
- Am Ende eines jeden *Topics* findest du einen **Test**. Mit diesen Aufgaben kannst du **überprüfen**, ob du die Grammatik beherrschst. Wenn du hier Fehler machst, solltest du dir die Erklärungen zur Grammatik noch einmal aufmerksam durchlesen und die Übungen später wiederholen.
- Im **Vokabelverzeichnis** kannst du unbekannte Wörter und wichtige unregelmäßige Verben nachschlagen.
- Die **Lösungen zu allen Aufgaben** findest du im *Key* am Ende des Buches.

Ich wünsche dir viel Spaß und Erfolg bei der Arbeit mit diesem Buch!

Paul Jenkinson

Topics and Worksheets

Alle *Topics* in diesem Buch beginnen mit einem Text und *Questions on the text.* Es folgen Grammatikerklärungen und Aufgaben, in denen du die neue Grammatik anwenden kannst, sowie Übungen zu den Bereichen *Vocabulary* und Schreiben *(Using your English)*. Am Ende eines jeden *Topics* findest du einen kurzen *Test.* Hier kannst du überprüfen, ob du die neue Grammatik verstanden hast und anwenden kannst. Bist du noch unsicher, dann solltest du dir die Grammatikkästen noch einmal genau durchlesen und die Übungen zu einem späteren Zeitpunkt wiederholen.
Du kannst dir die Reihenfolge, in der du die *Topics* bearbeiten möchtest, selbst aussuchen. Im Inhaltsverzeichnis kannst du nachsehen, in welchem *Topic* ein bestimmtes Grammatikthema behandelt wird. Beginne am besten mit den Themen, in denen du dich nicht so sicher fühlst oder die du gerade im Unterricht durchgenommen hast.

Topic 1: Sky City

The Native Americans are well known for their beautiful ceramics. There are many tribes and each one is different. One group lives in Pueblo Acoma, which is also known as Sky City.

Sky City is in New Mexico. It's a village on top of a 110 metre-high mesa: a mesa is a single high hill with a flat top. There wasn't a road to the village until the 1950s. The houses in the village belong to the women, and they are given from mother to daughter. There are about three hundred houses in the village.

The people in Pueblo Acoma paint their ceramics with fantastic patterns. These patterns usually have lots of thin lines and geometrical shapes which mean things: dots are rain and steps are clouds, for example, and often there are animal, insect and plant shapes, too. The inhabitants of Pueblo Acoma don't use many colours. The colours they use are normally only black, white, brown, red and orange.

Making something takes a long time. The clay has to be found, dug out of the ground, taken home and cleaned. After the clay has been prepared, a pot, for example, is then made by hand. The patterns are painted onto it with paints that are made from rocks and plants. Often a pot can take 60 hours to make. Finally, it's put in a very hot fire outside, or a kiln, in order to make it strong.

Vocabulary

ceramics (line 1): *Keramik*
clay (line 15): *Ton*
kiln (line 18): *Brennofen*
dot (line 10): *Punkt*
pot (line 15): *Topf*

Questions on the text

1 Do the tasks about the text. Sometimes you can tick (✓) a box and sometimes you have to write an answer.

a Only one Native American tribe is different.

This sentence is ☒ true

☒ false

because in the text it says ____________________

____

b What are the two names of the village?

The names are Pueblo Acoma / Sky City.

c Where is the village?

A ☒

B ☐

C ☐

d Which photograph shows the village?

A ☐

B ☒

C ☒

e A man cannot have a house in this village.

This sentence is ☒ true

☒ false

because in the text it says ____________________

____

f Which pattern is not one from this village?

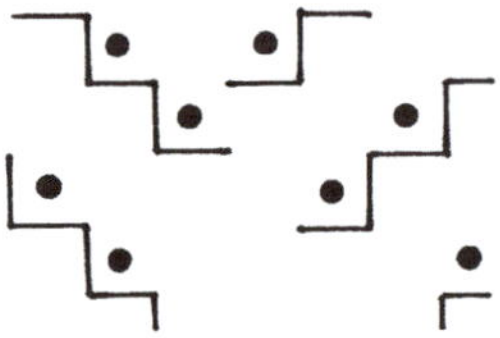

A [ ]

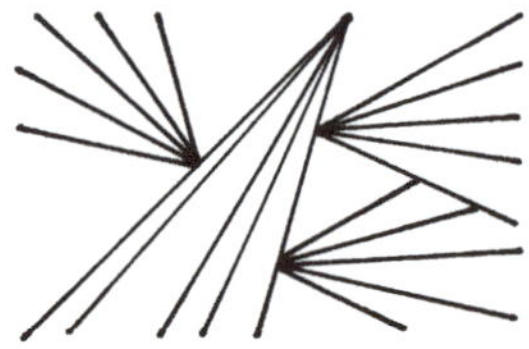

B [x]

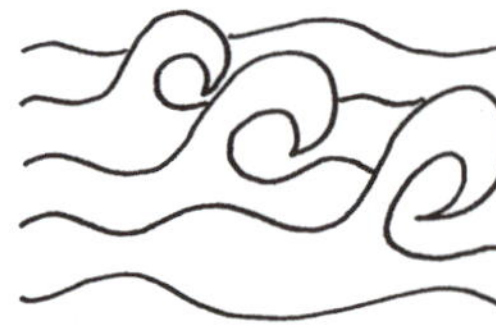

C [x]

g The typical colours used are red, black, white and blue.

This sentence is [ ] true
[x] false

because in the text it says black, white, brown, red and orange

h Tick (✓) the correct ending of the sentence.

The clay which is used …

- [ ] is bought in the next town.
- [x] comes from the mesa.
- [x] comes from a different area.
- [ ] takes a long time to be cleaned.

i Where do some colours come from?

A [ ]

B [x]

C [ ]

j Tick (✓) the two sentences that are true.

- [ ] Each pot takes sixty hours to make.
- [x] Some pots take sixty hours to make.
- [x] After the pot is painted it is put into a kiln.
- [ ] Before the pot is painted it is put into a kiln.

Grammar

Wann verwendest du das *simple present*?

Du verwendest das *simple present*:

- für **Gewohnheiten** und **wiederholt eintretende Ereignisse**.
  Signalwörter sind z. B. *every day, sometimes, always, often, never, usually, on (Mondays).*
  Beispiele: She collects ceramics.
  We often buy souvenirs on holiday.
- für **aufeinanderfolgende Handlungen**.
  Beispiel: First they fly to America. Then they drive to Sky City.
- bei **allgemeingültigen Tatsachen**.
  Beispiel: Water freezes at 0° Celsius.
- bei **Zustandsverben** (*state verbs*), da diese Verben normalerweise keine Verlaufsform (*progressive form* oder *-ing*-Form) bilden. Zu diesen Verben zählen z. B. *to be, belong to, have got, hate, know, like, love, need, want.*
  Beispiel: Sky City is a small village.
- für die **Zukunft**, wenn du über Fahrpläne, Sendungen, Termine oder Programme sprichst (***timetable future***). Normalerweise ist auch ein Signalwort der Zukunft nötig, z. B. *this evening.*
  Beispiel: The train leaves at 6 o'clock this evening.
- in **Nebensätzen der Zeit** mit Zukunftsbezug.
  Beispiel: I will read a book when I am on the train.
- in einem ***if*-Satz**, dessen Bedingung erfüllbar ist.
  Beispiel: If we go to New Mexico, we can visit Sky City.

Wann verwendest du das *present progressive*?

Du verwendest das *present progressive*:

- um auszudrücken, was zum Zeitpunkt des Sprechens **gerade passiert** und noch nicht abgeschlossen ist. Im Deutschen drückst du dies mit einem Adverb wie „gerade" aus.
  Signalwörter sind: *at the moment, now, just.*
  Beispiel: Look – he is making a pot.
- für die **Zukunft**, wenn du etwas schon **fest geplant** oder vorbereitet hast. Normalerweise steht auch hier eine Zeitangabe der Zukunft.
  Beispiel: We are meeting Tim at the station tonight.

2 Complete the sentences with the correct verb form.

be – be – close – go – like – take – visit – watch – write

a We sometimes ________________ a film at home in the evenings.

b Today we ________________ to Pueblo Acoma.

c If you ________________ New Mexico, you must buy something from the Native Americans.

d It ________________ very hot in New Mexico and Arizona.

e I ________________ an e-mail to my brother now.

f ________________ you ________________ the pot that I bought?

g It ________________ so warm today.

h Jo ________________ a photo of Sky City at the moment.

i The museum ________________ at 6 p.m.

3 Look at the photograph. Complete the sentences about it.

a Four people __________ on their horses.

b At the moment they __________ them. (not)

c One horse __________ anyone on it. (not)

d One man __________ next to a horse.

e I __________ the view.

f The people __________ at the view.

g Usually people __________ a lot of photos when they __________ here.

h The sun __________ today.

i I __________ the sun must shine here every day.

Vocabulary

4 Match the words to the correct picture. You might need some of these new words for the next exercise.

wavy line – straight line – curve – circle – dot – square – triangle – leaf shape – butterfly shape

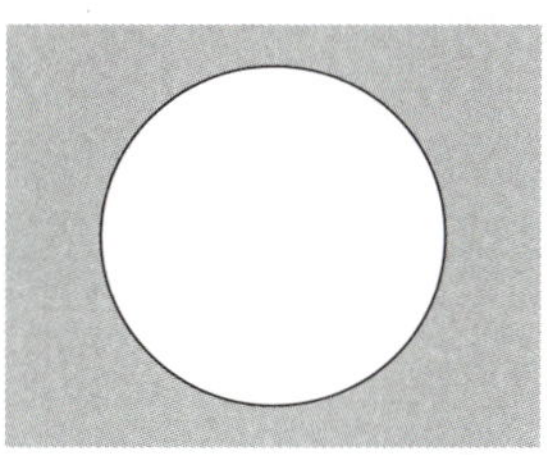

____

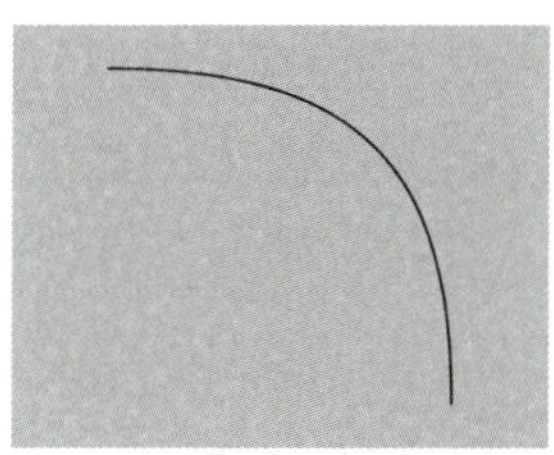

____

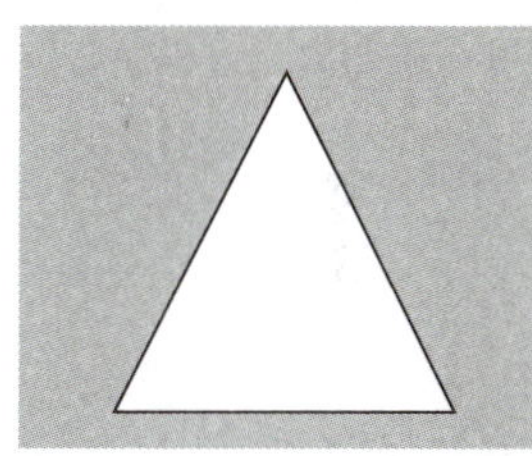

____

____

____

____

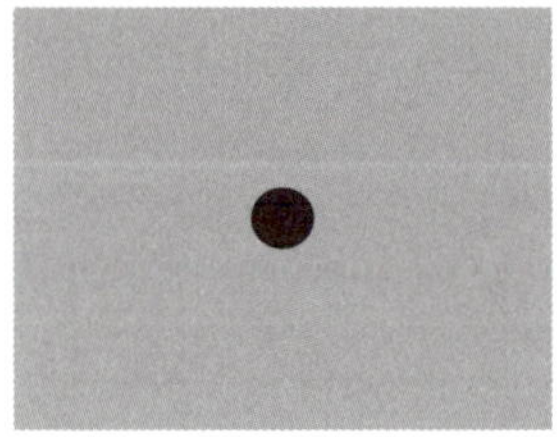

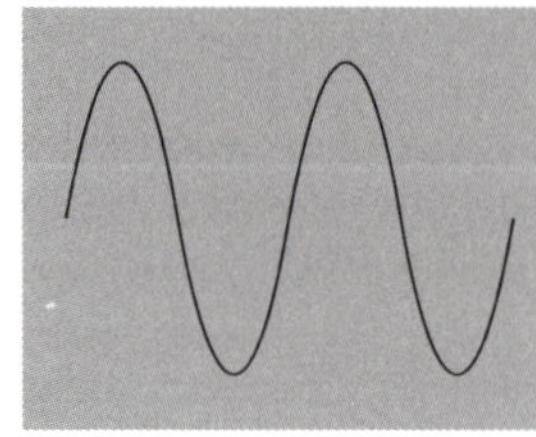

Using your English

5 You have just bought this pot at Sky City. Text a friend and describe it. You can use words from the text if you want to.

Hi Sally. I've just bought a great pot in Sun City. It's

Test

6 This is a story in three parts. Complete the sentences using the *simple present* or the *present progressive*. You are given the words you need but they are not in the correct order.

a *be – come – help – live – need – paint*

George ____________ from New Mexico. He ______________ a Native American and his family ______________ in Pueblo Acoma. At the moment George ______________ his sister, Andrea. She ____________ a beautiful pattern on a pot but she can't finish it – she ____________ more paint.

b *ask – use – visit*

When George ______________ his family, Andrea often ____________ him to find the plants and rocks she __________________ for the paint.

c *be – (you) do – leave – like – (not) make – meet – read – stay – travel*

George's best friend in Acoma is Mike. Mike __________________ pots, he makes jewellery.

"Hi, Mike. What __________________?" says George.

"I __________________ an interesting book about traditional jewellery," answers Mike.

"I __________________ that type of jewellery, too," says George.

"You don't normally _______________ this long, George," says Mike.

"That ______________ true," answers George. "But I ______________ Martina in Flagstaff on Wednesday and then we ____________________ home together. The train ___________________ in the afternoon."

Topic 2: Where's London Bridge?

Where's London Bridge? It's in a desert in Arizona, of course! And one man made it happen.

The story started in the 1930s when the Parker Dam was built across the Colorado River. Behind it the Colorado became a long thin lake. One day a rich businessman, Robert McCulloch, was on a peninsula in the lake. He thought that the area would be fantastic for water sports and holidays, and for people to live and work there. He decided to buy the peninsula and the desert land around it and build a city.

McCulloch's first houses were finished in 1963 but not many people wanted to live in Lake Havasu City. McCulloch soon found an answer to this problem: he opened three factories there which quickly brought a lot of people and their families to the city. He then got other businesses to come to the area, as well. But it was a new city and it needed something special in it.

In England, London Bridge was in a very bad condition. The City of London decided to build a new bridge and sell the old one. Robert McCulloch heard about this and bought the bridge for his new city. The stones from the bridge were taken by boat to Long Beach, California and then carried by lorries to Lake Havasu City, 300 miles away in the Mojave Desert. The bridge was then built on the narrowest part of the peninsula. After that, the land was dug away so that the peninsula became an island and in 1971 the bridge became a bridge again – and one of Arizona's main tourist attractions.

McCulloch had another plan for Lake Havasu City. He loved flying and dreamed of everyone having a small plane in their garage. He built the wide streets for the planes but no one wanted to fly to their holiday homes or hundreds of miles to work every day from the city.

Vocabulary

dam (line 3): *(Stau)Damm*
businessman (line 5): *(hier) Unternehmer*
peninsula (line 5): *Halbinsel*

Questions on the text

7 Read the text carefully; then answer the following questions. You do not have to write complete sentences.

View from London Bridge in Lake Havasu City

a Describe Lake Havasu.

The lake is ______________________________

____

b Who was Robert McCulloch?

____

____

c What did McCulloch think people could do on the lake?

____

____

d What did McCulloch do first?

____

e When were the first homes ready?

____

f Why were the factories important for the city?

____

g Why did the City of London want to sell London Bridge?

____

h How did the bridge get to Lake Havasu City?

____

i When was the bridge finished?

____

j Why were wide streets built in Lake Havasu City?

____

8 You have a task for each illustration. Draw your answer.
You are given an example (a).

a Show where the dam is and what happened to the river.

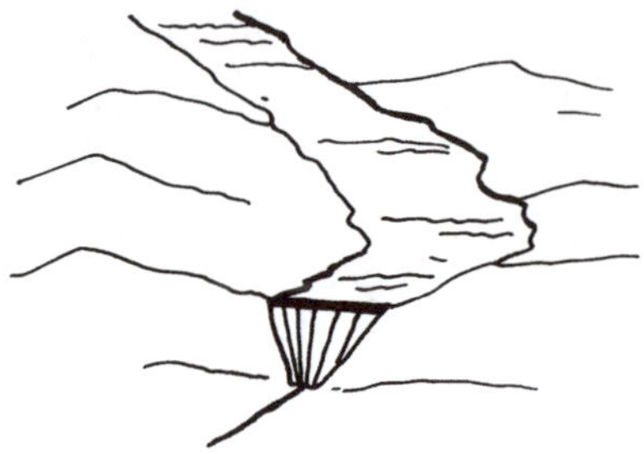

b Show the area that McCulloch bought.

c Show exactly where the bridge came from.

d Show how the bridge got to America.

e Show where the bridge went and what happened.

f Show another McCulloch idea.

Grammar

Wann verwendest du das *simple past*?

Du benutzt das *simple past*:

- für Handlungen und Zustände, die in der **Vergangenheit** liegen und bereits **abgeschlossen** sind.
  Signalwörter sind z. B. *yesterday, last (week/month/year), (three weeks) ago, in (2009), on (Monday), at the weekend* und das Fragewort *when*.
  Beispiel: He bought the bridge in 1968.
- für **aufeinanderfolgende Handlungen**, die **in der Vergangenheit** stattfanden.
  Signalwörter sind z. B. *first, then, after that, the next (day/month/year), (two days) later.*
  Beispiel: First he bought the land, then he built his city.
- bei **Zustandsverben** *(state verbs)*, da diese Verben normalerweise keine Verlaufsform (*progressive form* oder *-ing*-Form) bilden. Zu diesen Verben zählen z. B. *(to) be, belong to, have got, hate, know, like, love, need, want.*
  Beispiel: Only Robert McCulloch wanted the bridge.

Wann verwendest du das *past progressive*?

Du verwendest das *past progressive*, um auszudrücken, dass:

- eine Handlung **während eines Zeitraums in der Vergangenheit vor sich gegangen** ist.
  Beispiel: On Saturday, Linda was visiting the lake.
- eine **Handlung zu einem bestimmten Zeitpunkt** in der Vergangenheit **ablief**.
  Beispiel: At five o'clock, Linda was still talking on the phone.
- eine **Handlung gerade ablief** als eine **zweite Handlung einsetzte**.
  Beispiel: I was reading my book when Linda returned.

9 Complete the text that Sara sends to her aunt.

Hi Aunty Kathy,

Sorry – we Sw____________ *(swim)* when you phoned – never mind. We ____________ *(arrive)* yesterday after a long journey. While Mum ____________ *(drive)*, Dad ____________ *(sleep)* – typical! I ____________ *(stay)* in my room last night but Matthew ____________ *(go)* for a walk. He ____________ *(take)* photos of the bridge until 11 p.m.! He ____________ *(show)* me the photos before breakfast. While we ____________ *(eat)* breakfast, I ____________ *(remember)* that it was your birthday. Happy birthday from us. Love from everyone.

Wann verwendest du das *present perfect simple?*

Du benutzt das *present perfect simple:*

- für Handlungen und Zustände, die in der Vergangenheit angefangen haben und **bis in die Gegenwart andauern.**
  Beispiele: I have taken a photo to send to my friend.
  She has always loved America.
- für Handlungen, die sich **gerade eben** ereignet haben.
  Beispiel: We have just eaten breakfast.
- für abgeschlossene Handlungen in der Vergangenheit, die **Auswirkungen auf die Gegenwart** haben. Hier hat der Zeitraum oder der Zeitpunkt, zu dem eine Handlung stattfand, keine Bedeutung, weil du die **Ergebnisse** betonen willst.
  Beispiel: I've broken my glasses – I can't read anything.

Wann verwendest du das *present perfect progressive?*

Du benutzt das *present perfect progressive*, um zu beschreiben, dass eine Handlung in der Vergangenheit eine Zeit lang andauerte, sich bis in die Gegenwart erstreckt und auch noch in die Zukunft reichen kann. Du **betonst** also **die Zeitdauer**.

Beispiel: We have been driving all day.

Welche Signalwörter für das *present perfect* gibt es?

Signalwörter für das *present perfect* sind z. B. *already, ever, just, never, (not) yet, up to now, since* und *for*.

Was musst du bei der Verwendung von *since* und *for* beachten?

- ***since*** bezieht sich immer auf einen **Zeitpunkt** (z. B. *2008, Christmas, September, I was a child*).
  Beispiel: London Bridge has been a tourist attraction since 1971.
- ***for*** bezieht sich immer auf einen **Zeitraum** (z. B. *three days, a long time*).
  Beispiel: Harry has wanted to visit Lake Havasu for two years.
- Oft verwendest du nach *since* und *for* das *present perfect progressive*, um die Zeitdauer einer Handlung zu betonen.
  Beispiel: Mike and Kim have been flying for twenty minutes now.
- Wenn du aber das Ergebnis einer Handlung hervorheben möchtest, dann verwendest du das *present perfect simple*.
  Beispiel: Anna has played tennis since 2009. She's really good at it now.

10 Matthew and Sara are staying at a hotel in Lake Havasu City. What are they saying to each other? Write complete sentences using the information below and the *present perfect*.

a We – not eat – yet.

____

b Mum – not swim – this morning.

____

c I – just – talk to – Aunt Kathy – half an hour.

____

d I – not speak to her – Christmas.

____

e How long – you – wait?

____

f I – sit here – ten minutes.

____

g Dad – love boats – our holiday on one in France.

____

h He – want a boat – years.

____

Wann verwendest du das *past perfect*?
Das ***past perfect*** ist die „Vorvergangenheit". Es steht oft in Sätzen mit *after* und *before*. Du verwendest es,

- wenn eine **Handlung** in der Vergangenheit **vor einer anderen Handlung in der Vergangenheit** abgeschlossen worden war.
  Beispiel: After she had visited California she drove to Arizona.
- wenn ein **Zustand vor einem Zeitpunkt in der Vergangenheit** angefangen hatte.
  Beispiel: It had rained before we arrived.

11 Sara got a text back from her aunt. Complete the gaps in it and the ones in Sara's reply. Use the *past perfect* and the *simple past*.

Hi Sara,
After I ________________ (phone) you, I ____________________ (go) to the swimming pool, too. Thanks for the birthday wishes. How are you all? K.

Hi Aunty Kathy,
It ____________ (be) too hot to walk very far the day before but it ____________ (be) cooler this morning. So, after we ________________ (walk) across London Bridge we ______________ (go) to the lake. But by lunchtime we ________________ (see) everything and it ________________ (be) very hot again. We ____________________ (already/decide) to leave today so we just ____________ (leave) a few hours earlier. S.

12 Fill in the gaps in the following sentences. The verbs you need are in brackets.

a We ____________________ in America for ten days now. *(be)*

b My father __________________ a long way before we ____________________ to a bridge across the Colorado River. *(drive, come)*

c The river soon ______________________ a long, thin lake. *(become)*

d I ________________ boats on the lake and some people __________________ in it. *(see, swim)*

e People __________________________ in Lake Havasu City since 1963. *(live)*

f While we ______________________ to the bridge it ______________________ still 40 ° Celsius. *(walk, be)*

g I ______________________ to our hotel and ______________________ to the swimming pool. *(return, go)*

Vocabulary

13 Look at the photographs carefully. They were all taken in Venice Beach, Los Angeles.

- What is the subject of the photograph?
- Write three verbs and three adjectives or adverbs that have something to do with the photo.

a

subject: *a shop*

verbs: *sell, ...*

adverbs or adjectives: *colourful, ...*

b

subject: ______

verbs: ______

adverbs or adjectives: ______

c

subject: ______

verbs: ______

adverbs or adjectives: ______

d

subject: ______

verbs: ______

adverbs or adjectives: ______

Using your English

14 Imagine that you have been to Venice Beach in Los Angeles. Write an entry in your e-diary using as many words as possible from exercise 13 and the photographs.
Write at least **three** sentences about **each** photograph using forms of the past tense. A start has been made for you.

There were a lot of small shops near the beach. One of them was selling …

Test

15 Tick (✓) the correct box to complete each sentence.

a Yesterday we …
- ☐ bought
- ☐ have bought
- ☐ had bought

… some hats.

b After we …
- ☐ walk
- ☐ were walking
- ☐ had walked

… on the beach we …
- ☐ went
- ☐ have gone
- ☐ had gone

… home.

c The shop …	☐ hasn't been open ☐ wasn't open ☐ wasn't opening	… on Sunday.
d We …	☐ were shopping ☐ have been shopping ☐ had shopped	… all day last Saturday.
e They …	☐ were playing ☐ played ☐ have played	… music together for two years now.
f Up to now we …	☐ were ☐ were being ☐ have been	… here for a week.
g Joe …	☐ was surfing ☐ has been surfing ☐ had surfed	… since he was young.
h They …	☐ were driving ☐ drove ☐ had driven	… a long way before they saw the sea.
i In Hollywood Tom …	☐ has been imagining ☐ was imagining ☐ imagined	… himself as a film star.
j Three weeks ago I …	☐ have been walking ☐ had walked ☐ was walking	… along this street in the rain.

Topic 3: What's planned?

This year Sam is planning a holiday in America with his parents. Last week he told his friend, Becky, about his plan.
"We're going to go to America this year," Sam said.
"That'll be a great holiday," replied Becky. "I'd rather go with you than with my parents to the Lake District. How long will you be there?"
"We're going to be there for three weeks. We're leaving on the first Monday of the summer holidays and we're returning on the 23rd," explained Sam.
"Where are you going to stay?" asked Becky. "We're flying to San Francisco and then we're going to drive through California and five other states. I've been planning our holiday for months. It took a long time to organise. We're going to stay in lots of different places."
"Where are you flying from and how long is the flight?" Becky asked again.
"We're flying from London Heathrow," answered Sam. "It's quite a long flight. It takes over ten hours. I think I'll read a book on the plane."
"You'll probably just watch films," said Becky. "Last year we went to Hong Kong. That was a very long flight, too. I watched three films and slept for an hour and then I was in Hong Kong. I'm sure it'll be the same for you."

Questions on the text

16 Are the sentences *true*, *false* or *not in the text*?
Tick (✓) the correct box.

		true	false	not in the text
a	Sam is going to go to America with his friend, Becky.			
b	Becky thinks the holiday will be expensive.			
c	The holiday is for twenty-one days.			
d	Sam is flying at the start of the month.			
e	He is going to stay in some nice hotels.			
f	He is not flying from Germany.			
g	Sam is going to take books and magazines with him.			
h	When Becky flew, there was a bad storm.			
i	Sam's friend has been on a long flight, too.			
j	She couldn't sleep on the plane.			

Grammar

Wie kannst du im Englischen die Zukunft ausdrücken?
Im Englischen gibt es das ***going-to*** und das ***will-future***. Du kannst aber auch das ***simple present*** und das ***present progressive*** verwenden, um dich auf Zukünftiges zu beziehen. Welche Zeitform du benutzt, ist abhängig davon, was du ausdrücken willst.

Wann verwendest du das *going-to-future*?
Du verwendest das *going-to-future*,
- um **Pläne** und **Absichten** auszudrücken.
  Beispiel: Tomorrow, Sam is going to plan his holiday.
- wenn du sagen willst, dass ein Ereignis **bald eintreten** wird, da es dafür schon **Anzeichen** gibt.
  Beispiel: That's a four-star hotel. It isn't going to be cheap staying there.

Wann verwendest du das *will-future*?
Das ***will-future*** verwendest du, wenn du
- **Voraussagen** über die Zukunft und zukünftige Ereignisse machen willst, die man nicht kontrollieren oder beeinflussen kann.
  Beispiel: Sam's mum will be 40 in August.
- **Vermutungen** äußern willst.
  Signalwörter sind z. B. *maybe, perhaps, probably, (to) expect, (to) hope, (to) be sure* und *(to) think*.
  Beispiel: I hope we'll have a nice holiday.
- **spontane Entscheidungen** treffen willst.
  Beispiel: Becky: "Of course I'll text you."

Wann verwendest du das *simple present*, um Zukünftiges auszudrücken?
Du kannst das *simple present* verwenden, wenn du über **Fahrpläne, Sendungen, Termine** oder **Programme** sprichst (*timetable future*). Normalerweise ist hier ein Signalwort der Zukunft nötig, z. B. *in the afternoon, at (5 o'clock)*.
Beispiel: The film starts at 9.00.

Wann verwendest du das *present progressive*, um Zukünftiges auszudrücken?
Du verwendest das ***present progressive***, wenn du etwas schon **fest geplant** und **Vorbereitungen** dafür getroffen hast. Normalerweise steht auch hier eine Zeitangabe der Zukunft.
Beispiel: We're flying from London next week.

17 Complete each sentence with the correct form of the future. You are given a situation to use. Look at the example.

a *fest geplant und vorbereitet*

They are collecting their new car tomorrow. *(collect)*

b *Plan*

On Wednesday I ______________________ a film at the cinema. *(watch)*

c *spontane Entscheidung*

"Are you going into town? I ______________________ with you." *(walk)*

d *Fahrplan*

The train ______________________ at 16.30 this afternoon. *(arrive)*

e *Absicht*

I ______________________ a book this afternoon for Kim. *(buy)*

f *Voraussage*

It ______________________ soon. *(snow)*

g *Termin*

School ______________________ half an hour later tomorrow. *(start)*

h *Vermutung mit Signalwort*

I expect we ______________________ early. *(be)*

i *Plan und Absicht*

You've bought a big picture. Where ______________________ it? *(you, put)*

j *Vermutung mit Signalwort*

They ______________________ on the next train. *(probably, be)*

Vocabulary

18 *The Sirens of TI* is a musical. *Sirens* are 'verführerische Damen' and *TI* means 'Treasure Island'.
Look at the poster. Match each word from the poster to its meaning; then say what the word means in German.

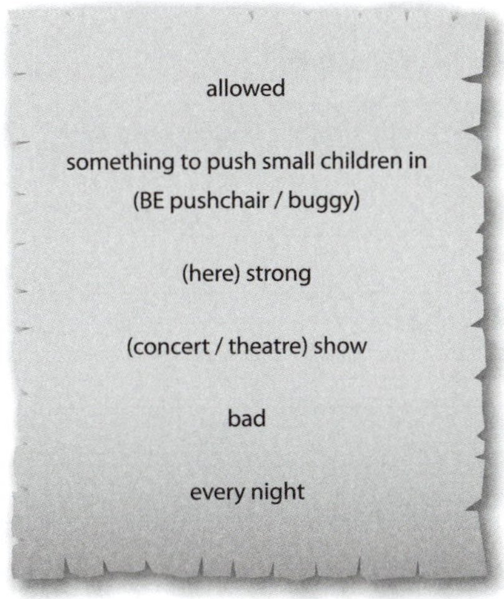

sign	meaning	German
nightly		
inclement		
high		
performance		
stroller	something to push small children in (BE pushchair / buggy)	
permitted		

Using your English

19 Text a friend and tell him or her about your plan to go to *The Sirens of TI* tomorrow night. Write six sentences using information from the poster and from each box.

sentence 1: tomorrow night	sentence 2: starts
sentence 3: hope / weather	sentence 4: expect / fun
sentence 5: little brother / walk / because	sentence 6: travel home / on Sunday

______________________,

____

____

____

____

____

____

____

____

____

See you soon,

____

Test

20 You are given three choices to complete each sentence. Read each sentence carefully and write down the best answer for it.

a We ______________________ to the concert in New York at the weekend. The tickets were quite expensive.

b I think ______________________ your holiday.

c My TV programme ______________________ in half an hour.

d What are your plans? ______________________ swimming tonight?

e ______________________ by train tomorrow, I've got the tickets already.

f It ____________________ dark by 6 o'clock tonight.

g "I ____________________ my bike later," she answered quickly.

h It ____________________ a super party, Jane has been planning it all week.

i You said that you would phone on Tuesday but when ________________?

j We ____________________ until 9 p.m. because of the bus.

k "Decide now!" Kevin said angrily. "____________________ me or not?"

l I ________________________ to the Lake District at the weekend to visit my parents.

m The plane ____________________ at 5 o'clock tomorrow.

n I'm sure I ____________________ very well tonight.

o We ____________________ a barbecue tonight.

a	will go	are going	are going to go
b	you are going to enjoy	you will enjoy	you are enjoying
c	finishes	will finish	is finishing
d	Will you go	Do you go	Are you going
e	We are going	We go	We will go
f	goes	is going to be	will be
g	will repair	am repairing	am going to repair
h	will be	is going to be	be
i	are you phoning	phone	will you phone
j	aren't arriving	won't arrive	aren't going to arrive
k	Help	Will you help	Are you going to help
l	am driving	drive	will drive
m	will land	is going to land	lands
n	am not going to sleep	won't sleep	am not sleeping
o	are going to have	will have	have

Topic 4: Hollywood

"We've got to visit Hollywood," Cindy said as they were walking along Venice Beach in Los Angeles. Jim wasn't too interested but he knew Cindy wanted to see all the famous sights. "OK, we'll go tomorrow if the weather is nice," Jim replied.
The next day Cindy said to the receptionist in the hotel, "Can we walk to Hollywood from here?" The woman in the hotel laughed and told them it was more than half an hour in the car – and then they would also need their car in Hollywood. She told them that if they had asked her the day before, they could have gone on a bus trip there that morning.
They drove to Hollywood and parked near the Walk of Fame. Jim was totally surprised. "I thought there were just a few stars' names here," he said. Cindy told him that the Walk of Fame had over 2000 stars' names along both sides of Hollywood Boulevard. Outside Mann's Chinese Theatre they saw where famous people put their hands and feet in concrete. Unfortunately, they couldn't see much because a film was being made there that day. They watched what was happening for about a quarter of an hour; then they walked further along the Boulevard and went into the Kodak Theatre where people get the Oscars.
Jim said, "Hollywood's interesting but it's not a very attractive place, is it?" Cindy replied that she would show him where the film stars lived and where they went shopping. They drove through Beverley Hills and saw a lot of famous people's houses.
"There's not a lot to see," complained Jim. He was very annoyed. "Just gardens, walls and gates!"
"You can see some people's houses – look at that one! If you don't like looking at famous people's houses, then I'll take you shopping. This is Rodeo Drive – the most expensive place to shop in L.A. If I lived in Beverley Hills, I'd go shopping here, too – all the top designers are here: Armani, Gucci and so on, and no prices in the windows! If you're extremely rich, you don't need to know the prices," explained Cindy.

Questions on the text

21 Read the text carefully. Tick (✓) the correct boxes, answer the questions and complete the sentences.

a Cindy and Jim went to Venice Beach and Hollywood on the same day.

This statement is ☐ true
☐ false

because ______________________________

____

b ______________________________, they would need about half an hour.

c If you walk along Hollywood Boulevard, what can you see?

A ☐

B ☐

C ☐

d Where was this photo taken and what is happening in it?

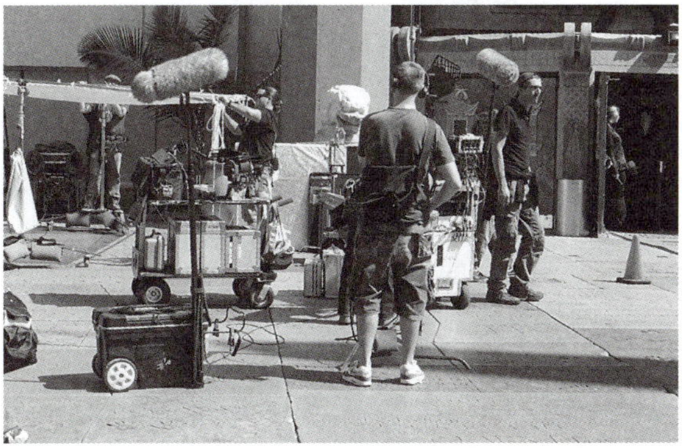

____

____

____

____

____

____

____

____

e In which building are the Oscars given?

A ☐

B ☐

C ☐

f What is Jim's opinion of Hollywood?

____

g Which house does Cindy probably see?

A ☐

B ☐

C ☐

h If you were a film star, where would you go shopping?

A ☐

B ☐

C ☐

i Why can't you see what things cost in the shop windows?

____

Grammar

Was sind Bedingungssätze?

Bedingungssätze ***(conditional sentences)*** bestehen aus einem Hauptsatz *(main clause)* und einem Nebensatz *(if-clause)*. Du kannst damit ausdrücken, **unter welcher Bedingung ein Ereignis eintritt**.

Die Reihenfolge von Haupt- und Nebensatz ist beliebig. Steht der Hauptsatz vor dem *if*-Satz, entfällt das Komma.

Beispiel: We might see someone famous if we go to Hollywood.

Wann verwendest du Bedingungssätze vom Typ I?

Du verwendest Bedingungssätze vom Typ I, wenn die **Bedingung erfüllbar** ist.

Wie bildest du Bedingungssätze vom Typ I?

- Im ***if-* Satz** steht das ***simple present***, im **Hauptsatz** das ***will-future***.
  Beispiel: If we walk, we will see more.
- Im **Hauptsatz** kann auch ein **modales Hilfsverb** (z. B. *can, must*) oder der **Imperativ** stehen.
  Beispiel: If I drive, we can be there in ten minutes.
- Wenn du eine **allgemein gültige Aussage** machen willst und die Folge immer dieselbe ist, ersetzt du das *will-future* durch ein Verb im ***simple present***. *If* bedeutet in diesem Fall *whenever*.
  Beispiel: If it is warm, she always wears a T-shirt.

Wann verwendest du Bedingungssätze vom Typ II?

Du verwendest Bedingungssätze vom Typ II, wenn die **Bedingung nicht erfüllt** werden kann oder es sehr **unwahrscheinlich** ist, dass sie erfüllt wird.

Wie bildest du Bedingungssätze vom Typ II?

- Im ***if*-Satz** steht das ***simple past***, im **Hauptsatz *would + infinitive***.
  Beispiel: If I visited Los Angeles, I would go to Hollywood.
- Du kannst *would* durch die **modalen Hilfsverben** *could* oder *might* ersetzen.
  Beispiel: If we asked that man, he might know the way to the Walk of Fame.
- Der Ausdruck „Wenn ich du wäre …“ lautet auf Englisch „*If I were you …*“.
  Beispiel: If I were you, I would buy a new car.

22 Match the stars together. Be careful – there are type I and type II conditional sentences in this exercise.

If we park here,

if we stand here.

If we lived here,

If I lived in Beverly Hills,

if we drive along this road.

If I had a Walk of Fame star,

If we go inside the Kodak Theatre,

We will be in a film

I would want it over there.

I would need a lot of money.

we can walk to the theatre.

we could go shopping in Rodeo Drive.

we can see where the Oscars happen.

We can take photos of the Hollywood sign

a *If we park here, we can walk to the theatre.*

b ______

c ______

d ______

e ______

f ______

g ______

23 Write the correct conditional sentences using the information in the boxes. If there is more than one answer, give the other possibilities, too.

a	*conditional sentence I*	be / sunny / tomorrow,	we / go / beach
b	*conditional sentence I*	you / be hungry,	buy / something / to eat
c	*conditional sentence II*	he / fly,	it / be expensive
d	*conditional sentence II*	you / like / rock music,	you / listen to / this band
e	*conditional sentence I*	hotel / be nice,	they / recommend it / to their friends
f	*conditional sentence I*	we / eat / now	we / not need / anything later
g	*conditional sentence II*	I / see / someone famous	I / ask / for an autograph

Wann verwendest du Bedingungssätze vom Typ III?

Mit einem Bedingungssatz vom Typ III beziehst du dich auf die **Vergangenheit**. Du drückst aus, dass die **Bedingung nicht mehr erfüllbar** ist.

Wie bildest du Bedingungssätze vom Typ III?

- Im ***if*-Satz** steht das ***past perfect***, im **Hauptsatz *would* + *have* + *past participle*.**
  Beispiel: If I had walked, it would have taken two hours to get there.
- Du kannst *would* durch die **modalen Hilfsverben** *could* oder *might* ersetzen.
  Beispiel: If we had arrived yesterday, we might have seen the concert.

24 Look at the small illustrations and then complete the type III conditional sentences.

a If I ______________________ in the film, I ______________________ an Oscar. *(act, win)*

b If I ______________________ on the wall, I ______________________ them making the film. *(stand, see)*

c If he ______________________ in America, he ______________________ English. *(live, speak)*

d If my computer ______________________, I ______________________ writing about Hollywood. *(not break down, finish)*

e If we ______________________ by bus, we ______________________ outside the theatre. *(go, get off)*

25 Use the information to complete the type III conditional sentences. The words in **bold print** need changing. Look at the example.

a Our football team **lost**, so I **didn't celebrate**. But …

If our football team had won, I would have celebrated.

b Julia's train **was early**, so she **didn't miss** the bus. But …

If Julia's train had been late, ______

c The sea **was cold**, so we **couldn't swim** in it. But …

______ *, we could have swum in it.*

d I **found** my camera and **took** a lot of photos of you. But …

______

e She **was ill**, so we **stayed** at home. But …

______

Vocabulary

26 Cindy and Jim drove to Hollywood and parked their car. They saw this sign in the car park. Match each word from the sign to its meaning.

1 instructions
2 key
3 space number
4 insert
5 desired time
6 display
7 receipt

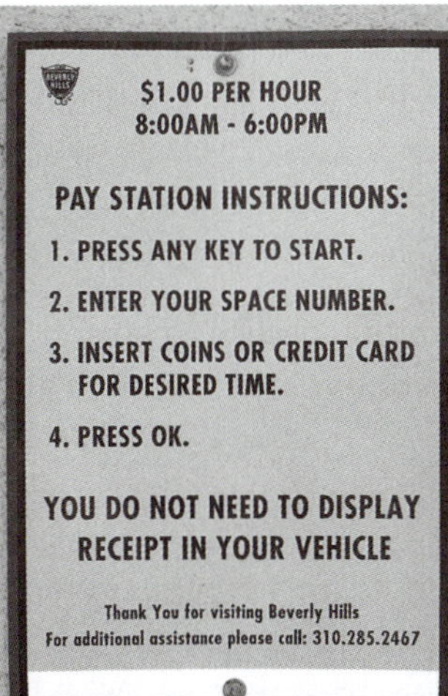

A the time that you want (to stay)
B the piece of paper that shows you have paid
C show
D how to do something
E a button you have to press
F put into
G the number on the wall or the floor where you have parked your car

1	2	3	4	5	6	7

Using your English

27 Imagine that you are Cindy or Jim. You meet some French tourists in the car park and they ask you some questions. Answer their questions in full sentences but make your instructions easy for them to understand. Use the information from the poster in exercise 26.

Tourist: Excuse me, do you know how much the car park costs?

You: ______________________________

Tourist: Where do I have to pay?

You: ______________________________

Tourist: How do I get a ticket?

You: ______________________________

____

____

Tourist: What do I do with the ticket?

You: ______________________________

Tourist: What happens if I have a problem with the parking meter at the pay station?

You: ______________________________

28 If you went to America, where would you like to go and what would you like to see? Write a small text with about five sentences in it and at least one conditional sentence.

____

____

____

____

____

____

____

Test

29 Look at the five photographs. Complete each type III conditional clause and say which photograph it is about.

a **Photo** ______: If I ____________________ the Redwood Groves, I ____________________ right. *(visit, turn)*

b **Photo** ______: If I ____________________ Malibu, I ____________________ 27 miles of scenic beauty. *(go to, see)*

c **Photo** ______: If I ____________________ east, I ____________________ on Route 66. *(drive, be)*

d **Photo** ______: If I ____________________ on the tribal roads, I ____________________. *(be, jog)*

e **Photo** ______: If we ____________________ here, we ____________________ a pizza. *(stay, buy)*

30 This is a mixed exercise with all three types of conditional sentences in them. Complete the sentences by ticking (✓) the correct box.

a If it had rained, I …	☐ won't go ☐ wouldn't have gone ☐ went	… for a walk.
b If we stay in this hotel, it …	☐ was ☐ will be ☐ might have been	… cheaper than the last one.
c If she goes by car, she	☐ will find ☐ wouldn't have to find ☐ may not find	… anywhere to park.
d If Jim hadn't seen me, he …	☐ will phone ☐ would phone ☐ would have phoned	… me.
e If we looked out of our window, we …	☐ could see ☐ can see ☐ could have seen	… the Hollywood sign.
f If we had walked, we …	☐ will be ☐ would be ☐ would have been	… here sooner.
g If you go to Hollywood, you …	☐ shall visit ☐ should visit ☐ should have visited	… Beverly Hills, too.

Topic 5: The park ranger

I would like to tell you about my job as a national park ranger. In 1832, an American artist, George Catlin, began a campaign to stop his people destroying their beautiful countryside and losing parts of their culture. He decided that Americans had better begin to look after some special areas. Just over thirty years later, Yosemite Valley in California became the first State Park, followed in 1872 by Yellowstone. But although the parks had begun and these areas were now protected, there was one very big problem; there was no one to look after them. That was why the national park rangers were introduced in 1916. The rangers now look after all the national parks and many other interesting places, too, for example the Statue of Liberty. Rangers work in 379 areas in almost every American state, and what is more, people love us for the work that we do.

Our main work is to make sure that the parks are safe for visitors and to give them information. We tell people about the place we look after and show them things. Rangers are also the policemen of the national parks: we have to fight fires, do repairs, and deal with emergencies. We can all give first aid and some rangers fly helicopters, too.

The cars we drive have special equipment in them so that we can deal with most problems, such as accidents, immediately, and we also carry brochures and maps to give to people.

The National Park Service also needs people to help them during the busy holiday periods. Temporary rangers do many different jobs from repairing signs and paths to collecting information about the park that they are in, for example about the plants, insects and animals.

If you want a job like mine or would like a summer job with us – phone 0924/456/6729 or go to www.nps.gov.

Vocabulary

first aid (lines 19/20): *Erste Hilfe*

(to) deal with (line 23): *(ein Problem/eine Situation) bewältigen*

temporary (line 28): *(hier) Aushilfs-*

Questions on the text

31 **a** Where can you find rangers working? Give two different examples.

____

b What isn't a ranger's job? Tick (✓) the correct box.

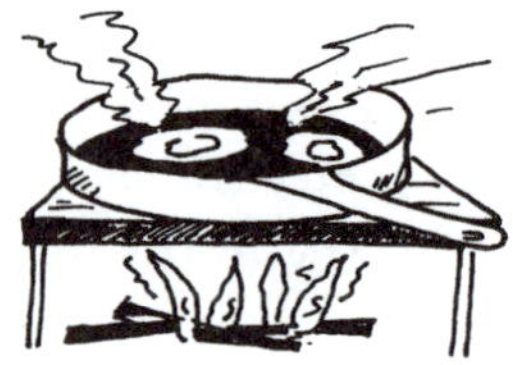

A ☐ B ☐ C ☐

c What was Catlin's aim?

____

____

d Why was the ranger service necessary?

____

____

e What can some rangers do? Tick (✓) the correct box.

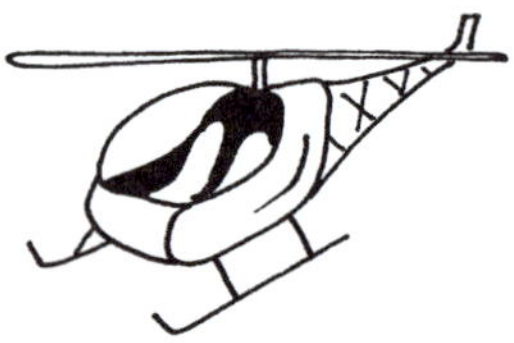

A ☐ B ☐ C ☐

f What can you find in a ranger's car? Answer in a full sentence.

____

____

g How can you find out more information about the rangers' work? Answer in a full sentence.

____

Grammar

Wie kannst du Zustimmung zu einer positiven Aussage ausdrücken?

Du kannst einer positiven Aussage zustimmen, indem du ***so* oder *too*** verwendest.
Im Deutschen drückst du deine Zustimmung durch „auch" aus.

Beispiel: I am staying in a nice hotel. So are we. *(Wir auch.)*
We are, too. *(Wir auch.)*

Was musst du bei der Bildung solcher Sätze beachten?

- Die Wortstellung in Sätzen mit *so* ist: ***So* + Hilfsverb/Form von (*to*) *be* + Subjekt.**
  Beispiel: Tony is from New York. So am I.
- Die Wortstellung in Sätzen mit *too* entspricht einem normalen **Aussagesatz.**
  Sie ist **Subjekt + Hilfsverb, + *too*.**
  Beispiel: Tony is from New York. I am, too.
- Enthält der positive Aussagesatz **ein Hilfsverb**, so wird dieses wieder aufgegriffen.
  Beispiele: She can swim far. So can Peter.
  Peter can, too.
  Jane has got a new car. So have I.
- Enthält der Aussagesatz **kein Hilfsverb/keine Form von (*to*) *be***, verwendest du eine **Form von (*to*) *do*.**
  Beispiel: They work in a national park. So does Tina.
  Tina does, too.

32 Use the words in brackets to agree with the statement.

a I find the ranger's job interesting.
(so – we) ______________________________

b Henry might look on their website later.
(so – Jane) ______________________________

c Today they are visiting the Statue of Liberty.
(too – Jason) ______________________________

d Anna comes from Germany.
(so – Fabian) ______________________________

e She wants to work in a bank.
(so – I) ______________________________

f David thinks he'll work in a shop.
(too – Gina) ______________________________

Wie kannst du Zustimmung zu einer verneinten Aussage ausdrücken?

Du kannst einer verneinten Aussage zustimmen, indem du ***neither, nor*** oder ***not … either*** verwendest.
Im Deutschen drückst du deine Zustimmung durch „auch nicht" aus.

Beispiel:	We aren't very happy.	Neither is Tom.	*(Tom auch nicht.)*
		Nor is Tom.	*(Tom auch nicht.)*
		Tom isn't either.	*(Tom auch nicht.)*

Was musst du bei der Bildung solcher Sätze beachten?

- Die Wortstellung in Sätzen mit *neither* oder *nor* ist:
  ***Neither* + Hilfsverb/Form von *(to) be* + Subjekt.** *oder*
  ***Nor* + Hilfsverb/Form von *(to) be* + Subjekt.**
  Beispiele: James can't play tennis. Neither can we.
  Nor can we.
- Die Wortstellung in Sätzen mit *not … either* entspricht einem normalen Aussagesatz. Sie ist **Subjekt + Hilfsverb/Form von *(to) be* + *not* + *either*.**
  Beispiel: Harry doesn't swim. Peter doesn't either.

33 You are given some statements. Explain what other people think about them. Use the words in brackets.

a Karen doesn't want to be a ranger.
(neither – Martin) ____________________

b They don't like beefburgers.
(neither – I) ____________________

c Sam isn't going to the party.
(nor – Lucy) ____________________

d They can't run very fast.
(nor – we) ____________________

e I couldn't get into the website.
(not … either – Linda) ____________________

f I wouldn't wear a uniform.
(not … either – he) ____________________

g Harry doesn't talk a lot.
(not … either – Jane and Tom) ____________________

34 Write about each photograph.

- The face shows if it's a positive ☺ or a negative sentence ☹.
- Write your sentence with the information you are given. Mind the tenses.
- You need to add names (e. g. Julie) or pronouns (e. g. he).

a

☺ like art – *simple present*

Mike likes art. So does Kylie.

b

☹ feed – *simple present*

c

☺ enjoy view – *simple past*

d

☹ be to the concert – *present perfect*

e

☺ have got a skateboard – *simple present*

Vocabulary

35 A park ranger is a fun job for lots of people. Do you know the names of some other jobs?

Krankenschwester/Krankenpfleger – Friseur(in) – Ingenieur(in) – Bauarbeiter(in) – Flugbegleiter(in) – Verkäufer(in) – Mechaniker(in) – Elektriker(in)

job	picture	German translation
builder		
electrician		
engineer		
flight attendant		
hairdresser		
mechanic		
nurse		
shop assistant / sales assistant		

36 What jobs would you like to do? Find out the English names for them.

Using your English

37 At the start of this chapter the ranger told you many things about his job. Imagine that you had to fill in this form for a job. What would you write in each section? Choose one of the jobs you wrote in question 36.

Name: ______________________________

Address: ______________________________

____

Tel: ______________________________

E-mail: ______________________________

Job: ______________________________

Why do you want this job? Answer in 30 – 50 words.

____

____

____

____

____

Write a profile about yourself. Write at least 50 words.

____

____

____

____

____

____

____

Test

38 The ranger, Luke, has given you a lot of sentences to complete about him, his work and people he meets. The words you need to make each sentence are in the brackets. He has given you an example to look at. You need only write one answer using the information.

a (I – enjoy – job / my friend Pete)

I enjoy my job. So does my friend Pete.

b (Greg – from America / Peter and Jane)

____

c (My brother – not swim / my sister)

____

d (Harry – drive – a lot / Mr and Mrs Smith)

____

e (Tricia – not like very hot weather / many people)

____

f (I – can – work – outside / Kim)

____

g (My dogs – big / yours)

____

h (We – not buy – house / our friends)

____

i (parents – are playing tennis tonight / I)

____

j (I – never – sad / wife)

____

k (I – not yet – be – to New York / my daughter)

____

Topic 6: Changing the world

Mark Zuckerberg

Mark Zuckerberg's website began on 4th February, 2004, while he was at Harvard University. It became very successful with the students there. Today, it is visited by millions of people around the world. Although there are many similar websites, Zuckerberg's is probably the best known one.

Martin Cooper

Everyone should know Martin Cooper but most don't. In 1973, he shocked many people in New York when he walked along the streets talking into a strange device. Like every new device, this one was big and heavy, about the size of a brick and two kilos. Cooper's invention is carried by most people today – now they are small and light, and simple ones are very cheap.

Vinnie Chieco

Do you know who Vinnie Chieco is? You probably don't but you will know the name he invented for a computer firm's product. In October 2001, Steve Jobs introduced this new device to the world, especially to young people so that they could listen to music everywhere. An online music store was also developed so that this product could work.

Johan Vaaler

Not everything that is great is new. In 1899 Johan Vaaler, for example, had a very clever idea. It was so clever that we still use it today and it hasn't been changed. Paper was a great invention but you could only tie pieces of paper together. In 1835, pins were invented for this but Vaaler made something out of metal which was much better.

Vocabulary

(to) tie: *(hier) binden*
pin: *Stecknadel*

Questions on the text

39 What did each person do or invent? Match the correct photo to the right person. There are more photos than you need.
Put the list in the correct time order, too.

(A)

(B)

(C)

(D)

(E)

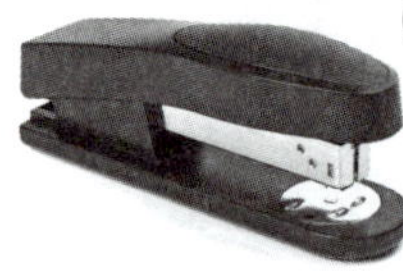

(F)

(G)

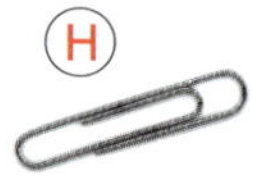

(H)

(I)

date	who	invention	photo

40 *True, false* or *not given?*

- ► Tick (✓) the correct box for each statement.
- ► Explain your **reason** for ticking *false* or *not given*.

	true	false	not given
a Zuckerberg was studying technology at Harvard University.	☐	☐	☐
Not given because ____________________			
b Students didn't like networking.	☐	☐	☐
____________________			
c One invention was tested outside.	☐	☐	☐
____________________			
d The size is still the main problem of Cooper's idea.	☐	☐	☐
____________________			
e Chieco invented the iPod.	☐	☐	☐
____________________			
f Online music stores are very successful.	☐	☐	☐
____________________			
g Vaaler's invention is still in its original form.	☐	☐	☐
____________________			
h Before 1835 pins were used to hold pieces of paper together.	☐	☐	☐
____________________			

Grammar

Worin besteht der Unterschied zwischen einem Aktiv- und einem Passivsatz?

- In einem **Aktivsatz** wird betont, **wer** (oder was) **etwas tut**.

  Beispiel: The students liked Facebook.
  (subject) *(verb)* *(object)*

- In einem **Passivsatz** steht im Vordergrund, **was getan wird**.
  Die Sache oder die Person, mit der etwas geschieht, bildet daher das Subjekt des Passivsatzes.

  Beispiel: Facebook was liked.
  (subject) *(verb)*

Wie bildest du das Passiv in den verschiedenen Zeitformen?

- Im ***simple present*** bildest du das Passiv mit: ***am / is / are + past participle.***
  Beispiel: Their products are improved.
- Im ***simple past*** bildest du das Passiv mit: ***was / were + past participle.***
  Beispiel: Their products were improved.
- Im ***present perfect*** bildest du das Passiv mit: ***has / have + been + past participle.***
  Beispiel: Their products have been improved.
- Im ***past perfect*** bildest du das Passiv mit: ***had + been + past participle.***
  Beispiel: Their products had been improved.
- Im ***will-future*** bildest du das Passiv mit: ***will + be + past participle.***
  Beispiel: Their products will be improved.

Wann verwendest du *by* in einem Passivsatz?

Manchmal ist es wichtig oder notwendig zu sagen, **wer etwas macht**. In einem Passivsatz kannst du den **Verursacher der Handlung** durch die Präposition ***by*** anschließen („*by-agent*").

Beispiel: Students used Facebook at first.

Facebook was used by students at first.

41 Read the following sentences carefully. Write them as passive sentences.

a Mark Zuckerberg started a successful website.

____

b New technology will make websites even more interesting.

____

c Martin Cooper shocked many people in New York.

____

d He introduced the iPod.

____

e Vinnie Chieco invented the name 'iPod'.

____

f The company developed an online music store.

____

g I will improve my presentation.

____

h Someone has used her paper clips.

____

In welchen Zeiten wird die Verlaufsform im Passiv verwendet?

Du verwendest die **Verlaufsform** *(progressive form)* im Passiv nur im ***present*** **und** ***past tense***.

Wie bildest du die *progressive form* im Passiv?

Du bildest die *progressive form* im Passiv mit: ***(to)* be + being + past participle.**

Beispiele:	The car	is	being	painted.	*(present progressive)*
	The bikes	are	being	washed.	
	The car	was	being	painted.	*(past progressive)*
	The bikes	were	being	washed.	

42 Use the passive to explain what is or was happening in each photograph.

a A map ______________________________

b A new shop ______________________________

c The view ______________________________ by many visitors.

d Yesterday, music ______________________________

e Last week, newspapers ______________________________ in the street.

f The car ______________________________ on a normal road.

Vocabulary

43 Match each English adverb to its German meaning.

teilweise häufig völlig seldom
selten partly
oft occasionally
gelegentlich completely
often frequently

German	English

44 Write each sentence using the passive and one of the adverbs from exercise 43. Use the information in brackets to decide which adverb is needed.

a Jason answered the question. *(but not all of it)*

The question was partly answered by Jason.

b Young people play sport. *(most of them)*

c The owners open the castle. *(but only on some weekends)*

d Many people send text messages. *(at least one an hour!)*

e The man drove the car. *(but only on some Sundays)*

f Jane did her work by herself. *(all of it)*

Using your English

45 Write a small article about the first flight *(Flug)*. Use the information you are given. Use the passive.

- first flight – made – 1903
- plane – called – The Flyer
- flown – Wright brothers
- first flight – completed – Orville Wright
- four flights – made – that day
- fourth flight – plane – flown – for 260 metres – Orville's brother

Test

46 Find four passive sentences in the texts at the beginning of this chapter: one from each part. Write them into the answer space.

a ______

b ______

c ______

d ______

47 Write the following sentences in the passive.

a The shop is repairing her mobile phone.

____

b People had used PCs for many years before laptops.

____

c The company will develop a new computer programme.

____

d Tom and Mike are using my camera.

____

e The drivers were driving their cars very fast.

____

f The boy was carrying a lot of books to the library.

____

g Her friends have seen her in the park.

____

h The school was sending e-mails to parents.

____

i People built the first cars a long time ago.

____

j Many young people enjoy chatting on the internet.

____

k The company liked the new car design.

____

l Jason was painting the house all day.

____

m The pupils have made a film about school.

____

Topic 7: Living with languages

Chinese is spoken by a much larger number of native speakers than English. However, it is English that has become the language used to communicate with in business in most countries around the world and a language that most people can speak.
A large part of the world has English as its native language but there are differences in it. As you already know, some American and British words are the same but are spelt differently. What you may not know is that the two countries also have some different expressions: a 'queue' in England, for example, is a 'line' in America.
English and all the other languages spoken around the world are so-called 'living languages', which means they change. In Britain, for example, a waiter would always say 'Enjoy your meal' or nothing at all when the meal is placed in front of you in a restaurant. Today you often hear the American expression 'Enjoy' when this happens.
Germans sometimes use English words, too, but they are often used differently. 'Handy', for example, is an English word but in English it doesn't refer to a mobile phone; it means *'praktisch'* or *'nützlich'*. There are also some German words which look and sound like English ones but have a different meaning. These are often called 'false friends'; for example, *sensibel* means sensitive (*empfindlich*) but there is an English word 'sensible' which means *vernünftig*. British people also use some German words: 'angst' and 'schadenfreude' are two examples. And sometimes you will even see signs with mistakes on them!
English is also used in India, together with Hindi, as an official language because the country is very big and has many languages of its own. In this way everyone there can understand each other. In the Indian communities in Britain you can often see examples of this on signs.
Finally, if you think that British people only speak English, you are wrong. If you look at Wales, for example, you will see that another language is often used there, too.

Vocabulary

(to) refer to (lines 16/17): *sich beziehen auf*
community (line 25): *Gemeinde*

Questions on the text

48 Answer each question. You do not have to write full sentences.

a Is the native language of most people in the world English?

___

b Why do people in other countries use English?

___

c Is English the same all over the world?

___

d Name two differences between British and American English.

___

e Why does English change?

___

f What does *'praktisch'* mean in English?

___

g What is a false friend?

___

___

h Name two German words that are used as English ones.

___

i Where can you find Hindi being used in England?

___

j Is English the only language you will find British people using?

___

k Which country also uses two languages?

___

49 Read the text again carefully and look at the photographs.

- Which photographs (1–9) match the statements a–e? Write the number of the photograph in the box.
- Which parts of the text match each statement (a–e) and its photo? Write that part of the text into the answer space.
- There are more photos than you need.

1

2

3

4

5

6

7

8

9

a	Photo:	Shopping in some parts of British towns
	Text:	
b	Photo:	Walking along an American street
	Text:	
c	Photo:	A business meeting in India
	Text:	
d	Photo:	This can't be correct, can it?
	Text:	
e	Photo:	A sign in a street in Wales
	Text:	

Grammar

Wie bildest du das Passiv bei Verben mit zwei Objekten?

Manche Verben haben ein **indirektes und** ein **direktes Objekt** bei sich. Das indirekte Objekt ist meist eine Person, das direkte Objekt ist in der Regel ein Gegenstand. Beide Objekte können zum Subjekt des Passivsatzes werden.

- Wenn das **indirekte Objekt** des Aktivsatzes **zum Subjekt** des Passivsatzes wird, spricht man von **persönlichem Passiv**. Denk daran, dass du die Subjektformen der Personalpronomen verwendest: *I – you – he, she, it – we – you – they*. Das direkte Objekt bleibt unverändert.

  Beispiel: Active sentence: Tina gave him (*ind. Objekt*) a nice present (*dir. Objekt*).
  Passive sentence: He (*Subjekt*) was given a nice present (*dir. Objekt*).

- Das **direkte Objekt** des Aktivsatzes kann ebenfalls **zum Subjekt** des Passivsatzes werden. Diese Form des Passivs ist seltener und hebt den Gegenstand im Vergleich zur Person stärker hervor. Das **indirekte Objekt** schließt du in diesem Fall **mit** der Präposition ***to*** an.

  Beispiel: Active sentence: Kim wrote my brother (*ind. Objekt*) a long e-mail (*dir. Objekt*).
  Passive sentence: A long e-mail (*Subjekt*) was written to my brother (*dir. Objekt*).

50 Read the following sentences. Write each sentence using the passive. In most sentences you are asked to give two answers.

a Lilly told me a story.

❶ ______________________________

❷ ______________________________

b They bought her a new mobile phone.

______________________________ *a new mobile phone.*

c We sent Tim an e-mail.

❶ ______________________________

❷ ______________________________

d Tom took them some pieces of cake.

❶ ______________________________

❷ ______________________________

e Someone stole Janet's bike at the supermarket.

____

f The teacher showed the children the website.

❶ ______________________________

❷ ______________________________

g Grandma lent us the money.

❶ ______________________________

❷ ______________________________

h I gave her the book.

❶ ______________________________

❷ ______________________________

i The visitors watched the film about Africa.

____

Wie bildest du das Passiv bei Verben mit Präposition/Adverb?

Im Passivsatz steht die Präposition oder das Adverb **direkt nach dem Verb**.

Beispiel: Active sentence: We were looking at the picture.
Passive sentence: The picture was being looked at.

Wie bildest du das Passiv mit modalen Hilfsverben?

Das Passiv mit modalen Hilfsverben (z. B. *can, must*) wird folgendermaßen gebildet: ***modal auxiliary + be + past participle.***

Beispiel: Active sentence: You can buy this book in the supermarket.
Passive sentence: This book can be bought in the supermarket.

Wann verwendest du Verben des Sagens und Denkens im Passiv?

Du verwendest Verben wie *(to) say, believe, know, suppose* und *think* im Passiv, wenn du ausdrücken möchtest, dass es sich um eine **weitverbreitete Meinung** oder ein **Gerücht** handelt, oder wenn die **Quelle** der Information **nicht genannt** werden soll. Im Deutschen drückst du dies durch das unpersönliche „man", durch das Hilfsverb „sollen" oder ein Adverb wie „angeblich" aus.

Beispiel: Sport is said to be good for you.
Sport soll gut für dich sein.

Was musst du bei der Bildung beachten?

- Die Satzstellung ist ***(to) be + past participle*** (z. B. *said/thought*) **+ to + infinitive.**
- Diese Konstruktion verwendest du meist im ***simple present.***

Beispiel: Active sentence: Many people think the music is too loud.
Passive sentence: The music is thought to be too loud.

51 Write each sentence using the passive. Before you start, look carefully at the tense so that you can use the correct form in your answer. If you have forgotten about passive tenses, look at page 48.

a They are looking at the view.

____

b Many people listened to the concert.

____

c The man was driving across the bridge.

____

d People know that flying is very safe.

____

e Everybody says surfing is difficult.

____

f People believe that English is an important language to learn.

____

g You can buy sweets at the shop.

____

h You may climb the trees in the park.

____

i You shouldn't run across the road.

____

52 Complete the text with the correct form of the passive.

Before I flew to America, I ________________ *(am told / was told / had been told)* by friends that some English words were different there.
When I arrived, I hired a car. Driving an American car ________________ *(was said to be / has been said to be / will be said to be)* easy but some signs ________________ *(were / should be / could be)* difficult for English people to understand. I found one – *'Ped xing'*. I sent a photo and a text message to a friend. "This sign ________________ *(is seen / is said to be seen / can be seen)* everywhere," I wrote. "What does it mean?" My friend wasn't sure so he asked a lot of people for their opinion, too. Two days later I got an answer, "… it ________________ *(is thought to mean / was meant / can be meant)* 'pedestrian crossing'."
I had a problem with my car one day, too. An American stopped and helped me. A few phone calls ________________ *(is made / were made / had been made)* and suddenly my 'problem' became an 'issue'! But my issue ________________ *(was dealt with / can be dealt with / was said to be dealt with)* very quickly and so I was happy again.

53 Look at the photos carefully. Write a passive sentence about each photo using the information you are given about it.

a

mustn't feed – animals

____

____

b

think – roller coaster – scary

____

____

c

taken off – car's wheels

____

____

d

say – Hollywood Bowl – famous

____

____

Vocabulary

54 **a** Look at the following list. There are seven German words and then those words are in British English and American English. Match three words together, for example *pavement – Bürgersteig – sidewalk*. Write them into the correct illustration.

Autobahn
Eisenbahn
Gehsteig
Handy
Müll
Parkplatz
U-Bahn

car park
cell phone
freeway
garbage
mobile phone
motorway
parking lot
pavement
railroad
railway
rubbish
sidewalk
subway
Underground

b Look at the photos. Where does each of them come from – America or Britain? You can't say where one photo comes from – which one?

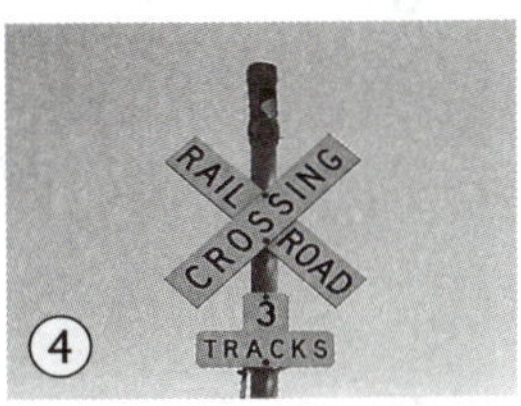

from Britain:

from America:

can't say:

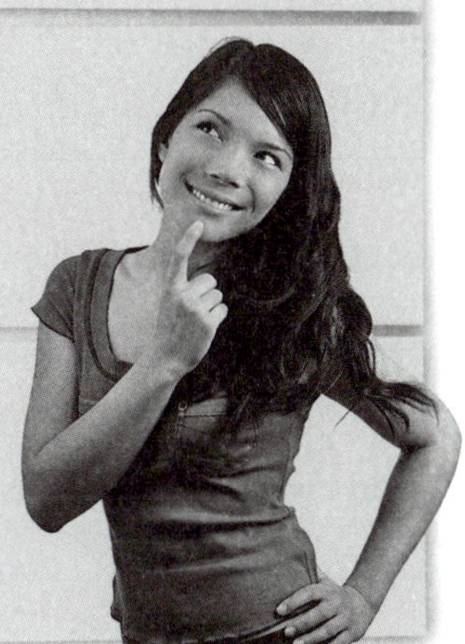

Using your English

55 Complete the story using the illustrations. Use British English or American English, but **do not use both**. Sometimes you have to use the passive, too.

Chris and Mandy took **(a)** ______________________ to **(b)** ______________________ station. Yesterday, their car **(c)** ______________________ in **(d)** ______________________ there by their parents. At the station they walked along **(e)** ______________________ until they came to it. They got into their car and then **(f)** ______________________ to **(g)** ______________________. The roads **(h)** ______________________ busy on Saturdays but this one wasn't. Mandy's **(i)** ______________________ didn't work because the battery was empty so their parents **(j)** ______________________ ______________________ on the way home.

Test

56 Write the following sentences using the passive. If there is more than one answer possible, give both variations.

a They gave him a nice present.

____

____

b Tom is looking at the picture.

____

____

c Many people believe the film is a true story.

____

____

d Jane can walk on the grass.

____

____

e The thief broke into the house.

____

____

f We must phone Peter later.

____

____

g All my friends say that this pop group is very good.

____

____

h Most people think driving is easier than flying.

____

____

Topic 8: Sport and leisure

Justine: Hi, Chang. Have you seen the advert in the newspaper about the new sports centre?

Chang: No, I haven't.

Justine: It sounds really good. There's an open day – days really – I want to go and have a look. Will you come, too?

Chang: I'm not sure.

Justine: I'll scan the advert and send it to you – think about it and phone me later.

Chang: Okay.

Later that day Chang read the advert that Justine had e-mailed him.

TRAFALGAR SPORTS

Trafalgar Sports is a new centre. We have three halls for indoor activities. Outside, we can offer many water sports on our private lake and river. We also have a climbing wall, outdoor go-karting and mountain bike tracks. Come along to one of our open days and look for yourself.

Open days: **Saturday, 4th June – Sunday, 5th June**

Times: **8 a.m. – 9 p.m.**

Courses: 60 minutes / 2 hours for mountain biking, sailing and windsurfing

Book:
- telephone: 0239/1111
- website: www.trafalgarsports.com
- e-mail: trafalgarsports@sommerton.com

Courses available: squash, tennis, badminton, swimming, golf, horse riding, go-karting, climbing, mountain biking, windsurfing and sailing – or try out our fitness studio.

See you at the weekend!

TRAFALGAR SPORTS • Holly Farm, Old Lane Road, Sommerton

Vocabulary

open day (line 4): *Tag der offenen Tür*

Questions on the text

57 Tick (✓) the correct answer box or write a short answer.

a Where was the information about Trafalgar Sports?

A ☐

B ☐

C ☐

b The open days are …

☐ next weekend.
☐ during the week.
☐ at a weekend.

c What is Justine going to do first?

A ☐

B ☐

C ☐

d Put the sports from the advert into the following lists. Write each sport only once.

- indoor sports ______________________________

____

- outdoor sports ______________________________

____

- both ______________________________

e How many hours each day is the centre open for?

____

f How long are the longest courses?

____

g How many ways are there to book a place on a course?

____

h Which sport can't you do at Trafalgar Sports?

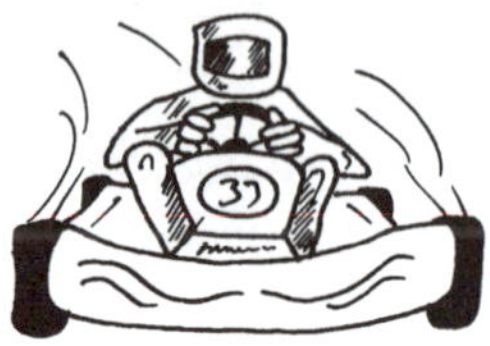

A ☐

B ☐

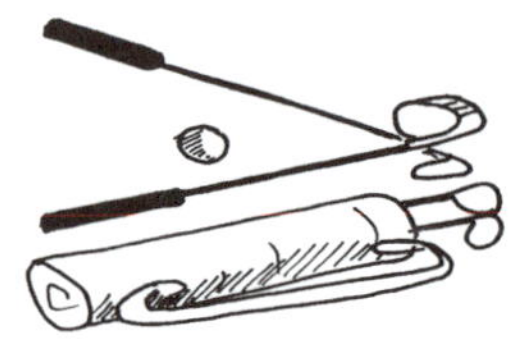

C ☐

Grammar

Was versteht man unter „indirekter Rede"?

In der direkten Rede macht ein Sprecher eine Äußerung. In der indirekten Rede **berichtet** ein Sprecher, **was eine andere Person gesagt hat**.

Beispiel:	*Sandy:*	My name is Sandy.	*(direkte Rede)*
	Lucy:	She said her name was Sandy.	*(indirekte Rede)*

Wie bildest du die indirekte Rede?

- Du beginnst die indirekte Rede mit einem **Verb der Mitteilung + *that***. Verben, die die indirekte Rede einleiten können, sind z. B. *(to) say, answer, write* und *explain*. *That* kann auch weggelassen werden.
  Beispiel: I wrote (that) I was going to England.
- In der indirekten Rede steht **kein Komma**.
- Du kannst die indirekte Rede auch durch *(to)* ***tell someone*** *(**that**)* einleiten. Beachte, dass du hier eine **Person** *(someone)* **nennen** musst.
  Beispiel: *Julia:* The book is over there. *(direkte Rede)*
  Julia tells Simon that the book is over there. *(indirekte Rede)*
- In der indirekten Rede werden die **Pronomen, Orts- und Zeitangaben** der direkten Rede verändert.
  Beispiel: *Larry:* I'm playing tennis here next week.
  He said he was playing tennis there the following week.
- Auch die **Zeitform** des Verbs kann sich verändern.
  Beispiel: *Paula:* She went to school in America.
  She said she had gone to school in America.

Was musst du bei den Zeitformen in der indirekten Rede beachten?

- Wenn das **einleitende Verb im *present tense, present perfect* oder Futur** steht, **bleibt das Verb in derselben Zeitform** wie in der direkten Rede.

Beispiel:

direct speech	reported speech
Jane: I sing in the bath.	She *says* she sings in the bath. She *has said* she sings in the bath.

- Wenn das **einleitende Verb im *past tense*** steht, dann wird das Verb der direkten Rede verändert. Es wird **um eine Zeitstufe zurückgesetzt**.

Beispiele:

direct speech	reported speech
present tense *Joe:* We are in London. *Joe:* We are visiting London.	**past tense** Joe *said* they were in London. Joe *said* they were visiting London.
past tense *Joe:* We were in London. *Joe:* We were visiting London.	**past perfect** Joe *said* they had been in London. Joe *said* they had been visiting London.
present perfect *Joe:* We have visited London. *Joe:* We have been visiting London.	**past perfect** Joe *said* they had visited London. Joe *said* they had been visiting London.

58 Write the following sentences in reported speech. To help you, the introductions in the past tense are in **bold print**.

a Manny: "Justine has just finished reading the advert."

Manny says ______________________________

b Jason: "Martin ran to the shop."

Jason told Chang ______________________________

c Owen: "I have been swimming."

Owen wrote ______________________________

d Tina: "We were playing golf."

Tina writes ______________________________

e Martin: "I'm in the garden."

Martin said ______________________

f Rachel: "Trevor has gone home."

Rachel tells Mike ______________________

g Arthur: "Carol loves horses."

Arthur said ______________________

59 Write the teenagers' direct speech as reported speech. Remember the tense changes. Use the introduction words in this order: *~~writes~~ – answers – told Geoff – said – wrote – explained – says – tells Justine — tells everyone.*

a *Justine writes (that)* ______________________ *horse riding.*

b *Chang* ______________________

c *Suki* ______________________

d *Harry* ______________________

e *Maria* ______________________

f Leo

g Justine

h Chang

i Suki

Wie bildest du die indirekte Rede mit modalen Hilfsverben?

- Die modalen Hilfsverben ***could, should, would, might*** und ***ought to*** **ändern** in der indirekten Rede ihre **Form nicht**.

Beispiel:

direct speech	reported speech
Felix: I would like an ice cream.	Felix *says* he would like an ice cream. Felix *said* he would like an ice cream.

- Folgende modale Hilfsverben musst du **verändern**, wenn das einleitende Verb im ***past tense*** steht: ***will, can, may, must / have to***.

Beispiele:

direct speech	reported speech
will *Tom:* I will read the book.	**would** Tom *said* he would read the book.
can *Tom:* I can read the book.	**could** Tom *said* he could read the book.
may *Tom:* I may read the book.	**might** Tom *said* he might read the book.
must / have to *Tom:* I must read the book. *Tom:* I have to read the book.	**had to** Tom *said* he had to read the book.

60 **a** Justine sent Chang a text message. Explain what she wrote.
Write each sentence with a different verb to start it, for example: *wrote, told, said …*

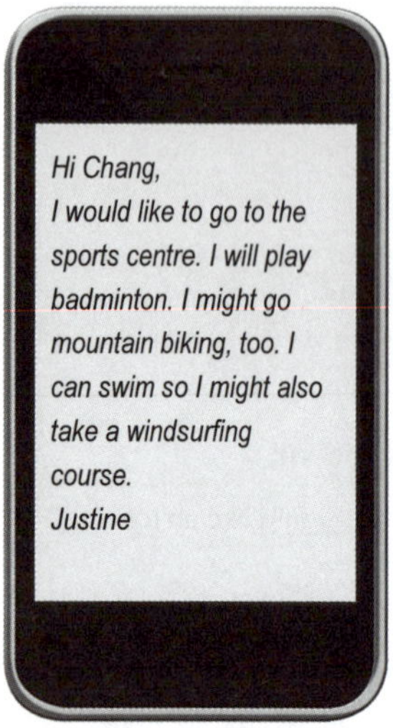

Justine wrote ______________________________
____
____
____
____
____
____
____
____
____
____

b Chang's reply: Explain what he wrote.
Write each sentence with a different verb to start it, for example: *wrote, told, said …*

Chang explained (that) ______________________________
____
____
____
____
____
____
____
____
____
____

Vocabulary

61 Prefixes are letters like *dis-*, *il-*, *im-*, and *un-* that go in front of some words to make new ones. Here are some tips on which ones to use with the following words. All of them make **the opposite** of the basic word.
For example: *tidy* ↔ *untidy (= not tidy)*

Tips	
dis-	makes the opposite of something – but this opposite is a change without a negative meaning. For example: *allow – disallow*
il-	often goes in front of words starting with 'l'
im-	is used with words starting with an 'm' or a 'p' and means 'not'
un-	gives the opposite of the basic word in a negative way

Using the tips make the opposite word for each of the following ones:

happy ↔ ________________

perfect ↔ ________________

agree ↔ ________________

clear ↔ ________________

possible ↔ ________________

advantage ↔ ________________

legal ↔ ________________

62 Write the opposite of each sentence by using the correct prefix on the right word.

a The children were very mature *(reif)*.

____

b The bridge was safe.

____

c The man connected the electricity.

____

d The question was logical.

____

Using your English

63 Read the story. Explain what Justine's mum told the policeman. Complete the report she gave.

Justine's mum decided to take her daughter and some of her friends to the open day because she has got the biggest car. Everyone jumped into it and they drove away. In the middle of the town the car suddenly stopped. "Oh, no. Get out and push," said Justine's mum.
Everyone got out of the car and pushed it to the side of the road. They were lucky because there was somewhere to park. Justine's mum got out of the car and looked at the engine.
"Mum, look here. There's water on the road and it's coming from our car," said Justine.
"I'm sorry, everyone. No open day today!" she said. Then she picked up her mobile and phoned a garage for help. Just then a policeman arrived and asked Justine's mum what her problem was.

Justine's mum explained ______________________________

to an open day. She then told him that everyone ______________________________

______________________________ but then the car

______________________________. She explained that

______________________________.

They ______________________________ to park.

She told the policeman there ______________________________

____

and that she ______________________________ a garage on her mobile.

Test

64 Write the sentences using reported speech.

a "We must learn to swim."

Tricia said ______________________________

b "There is a new sports centre."

Tony told Mike ______________________________

c "I may wash the car."

Mrs Jones said ______________________________

d "Jan is playing tennis."

Jason wrote ______________________________

e "I know because I've just seen Jan at the sports centre."

Melissa answered ______________________________

f "I would read the newspaper but I can't find it."

Mr Smith said ______________________________

65 Write Kim's text in reported speech.

> Hi Mark,
>
> I'm having a rest because I've just been riding my mountain bike. I've been along some great tracks. Some are easy and others are really hard and there's a river to cross without a bridge. I'm very wet. Meet me at the café in 10 minutes.
>
> Love,
> Kim

Kim wrote ______________________________

because ______________________________.

She said ______________________________.

She told Mark ______________________________

and ______________________________.

She complained ______________________________.

She suggested ______________________________.

Topic 9: Hungry?

Hungry? Why not try something from England? It's quick and easy to make and tastes good, too. You can add the things you like to it as well. Everyone makes jacket potatoes differently but here's one recipe to try.

I often have prawns with my jacket potato instead of the tuna. English people buy these fresh but you can get a packet of frozen ones at any supermarket. You don't need to cook them – just defrost them first. Take a nice handful and mix together with a small amount of mayonnaise. Instead of the tuna put the prawns and mayonnaise on the potato half.

Vocabulary

(to) grate: *reiben*
prawn: *Garnele*
cheddar/Gouda: *Käsesorten*
(to) defrost: *auftauen*

Questions on the text

66 Answer the following questions about the recipe. You do not have to write full sentences.

a Where does the recipe come from and what is its name?

____

b What do you have to do first to your potato?

____

c Why do you need a fork?

___

d How long does a potato take to cook in the microwave?

___

e Name the four ingredients that you need for the main recipe.

- ___
- ___
- ___
- ___

f Which two ingredients are not easy to get in Germany?

- ___
- ___

g Put the photos into the text order and write 1–4 in the boxes. Show which part of the text the photos come from: write the words from the text.

☐ ___

☐ ___

☐ ___

☐ ___

Grammar

Welche Änderungen können sich bei Pronomen in der indirekten Rede ergeben?

Personal- und Possessivpronomen der direkten Rede ändern sich, wenn ein Sachverhalt von einem **anderen Sprecher** in der indirekten Rede wiedergegeben wird.

Beispiele:

direct speech	reported speech
Peter: It's my car. *Sue:* We are going to the cinema.	*Joe:* Peter said (that) it was his car. *Joe:* Sue said (that) they were going to the cinema. **Aber:** *Sue:* I said (that) we were going to the cinema.

67 Write each sentence of the dialogues as reported speech. Look carefully at the introductory verb and the tense it has got.

a

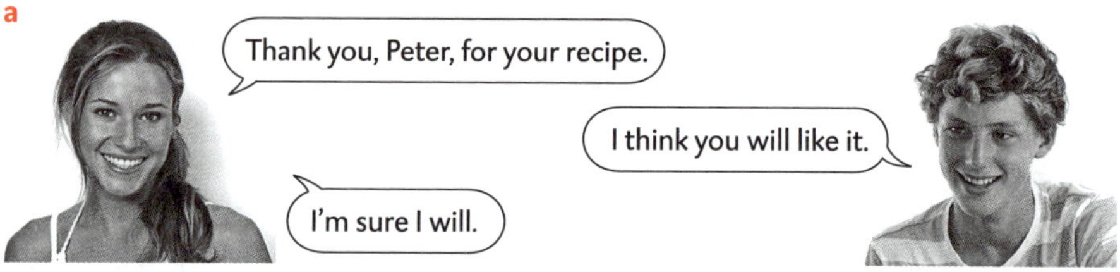

- Anna thanks Peter for ____________ recipe.
- Peter thinks ____
- Anna says ____

b

- Marcia says ____
- Tom replies ____

c

My mum wants me to go to the shop for her.

You can come with us.
We are going to the shop, too.

- Harry told Noah ______________________________
- Noah replied ______________________________

d

Our new neighbours are very nice.

I've spoken to them already.

- Gina told Sammy ______________________________
- Sammy said ______________________________

Was musst du bei den Zeitangaben in der indirekten Rede beachten?

- Die **Zeitangaben** bleiben in der indirekten Rede **unverändert**, wenn noch **am selben Tag**, in derselben Woche, in demselben Monat etc. berichtet wird.
  Beispiel: August 12th: *Peter:* I am washing my car today.
  August 12th: *Rita:* Peter has said (that) he is washing his car today.
- Die **Zeitangaben ändern sich,** wenn der Bericht zu einem **späteren Zeitpunkt** erfolgt, also z. B. am nächsten Tag oder eine Woche später.
  Beispiel: August 12th: *Peter:* I am washing my car today.
  August 13th: *Rita:* Peter said (that) he was washing his car yesterday.
- **Häufige Änderungen** bei den Zeitangaben sind:

direct speech		**reported speech**
now	→	then, at that time
today	→	(on) that day, yesterday, last (Friday)
yesterday	→	the day before, last (Friday)
last week	→	the week before
four months ago	→	four months earlier
tomorrow	→	the next day, the following day, on (Friday)
next week/year	→	the following week/year

Was musst du bei den Ortsangaben in der indirekten Rede beachten?
Welche Ortsangabe du verwendest, hängt davon ab, **wo sich der Sprecher** im Moment **befindet**.

Beispiel: *Jackie:* It is very nice here.
Jackie says (that) it is very nice there. *(Der Sprecher ist an einem anderen Ort.)*

Häufige Änderungen bei den Ortsangaben sind:

direct speech		**reported speech**
here	→	there
this / these	→	that / those

68 Hungry? Read what the two young people say about their lives.

- Write each sentence as reported speech.
- Write introductory words in the past tense: try to use different ones and not just *"said"*.
- The words in *italics* need to be changed in reported speech.

This is what **Ntila** says:

a "*I live* in Kenya and *yesterday we didn't have* anything to eat."

b "Every morning *here we collect* water before going to school."

c "*Today I haven't had* any breakfast."

d *"Last week our* goat *died."*

e "*This is* a big problem for *our* family."

a ______________________________

____

b ______________________________

____

c ______________________________

____

d ______________________________

____

e ______________________________

____

This is what **Jack** says:

f "*I live* in Britain and *we* never *have* any problems with food *here*."

g "*I was* hungry *yesterday*."

h "*My* mum *went* shopping *last Friday*."

i "*Tomorrow we are going* to a nice restaurant."

j "*Today we are having* fish and chips for dinner."

f ______________________________

____

g ______________________________

h ______________________________

i ______________________________

____

j ______________________________

____

Wie bildest du Fragen in der indirekten Rede?

- Die **häufigsten Verben**, die eine indirekte Frage einleiten, sind *(to) ask*, *(to) want to know* und *(to) wonder*.
- Wenn die direkte Rede ein Fragewort (z. B. *how, what, when, where, who, whose* oder *why*) enthält, **bleibt das Fragewort** in der indirekten Frage erhalten.

Beispiele:

direct speech	reported speech
Greg: Where is my coat? *Jenny:* Why are we waiting?	Greg asked where his coat was. Jenny wanted to know why they were waiting.

- Bei einer **Frage ohne Fragewort** steht in der indirekten Frage anstelle des Fragewortes ***if* oder *whether***.

Beispiel:

direct speech	reported speech
Jane: Is Mike going to the party?	Jane asked if/whether Mike was going to the party.

- Die **Wortstellung** in einer indirekten Frage **entspricht** der Wortstellung in einem **Aussagesatz**. Das Subjekt steht also vor dem Verb. Vor dem Subjekt steht **keine Umschreibung mit** *(to) do*.

Beispiele:

direct speech	**reported speech**
Lucy: How do we get to L.A.? *Mike:* Do you often go to L.A.?	Lucy asked how they got to L.A. Mike asked if/whether she often went to L.A.

- Die Regeln über die Veränderung der Zeitformen, der Pronomen, Orts- und Zeitangaben gelten auch hier (siehe Seite 69, 71, 79, 80).

Beispiel:

direct speech	**reported speech**
Freddie: Do you have your parties here?	Freddie asked if/whether they had their parties there.

- In der indirekten Frage steht **am Ende ein Punkt** und kein Fragezeichen.

69 Jack wants to know more about Ntila and how her family lives. Explain what he asked Ntila. Use as many different introductory words as possible. Write them in the past tense.

a How many people are in your family?

Jack wanted to know ______________________

b Do you have to walk to school?

____

c What do you eat?

____

d Where do you collect the water from?

____

e Why doesn't your family buy a new goat?

____

f Have you got a bike?

____

g Is it warm where you live?

____

h Do you live in a village?

____

i Who looks after the animals?

____

j When do you go to school?

____

Ntila also wanted to know more about Jack's life. Explain what she asked, too.

k Do you live in a big city?

____

l Why were you hungry yesterday?

____

m Are there a lot of shops near your house?

____

n What is a restaurant? We don't have any.

____

o When do you eat?

____

Wie bildest du Befehle und Bitten in der indirekte Rede?

- Die häufigsten **einleitenden Verben** für Befehle und Bitten sind *(to) tell, order, ask, advise* und *(to) warn.*
- Die **Satzstellung** in indirekten Befehlen und Bitten ist:
  Subjekt + einleitendes Verb + Objekt + *(not)* ***to*** **+ Infinitiv** …

Beispiele:

direct speech	reported speech
Geoff: Phone me later.	Geoff told Karen to phone him later.
Lucy: Don't play on the grass.	Lucy told her children not to play on the grass.
Amanda: Could you close the window, please?	Amanda asked her friend to close the window.

70 Do the following tasks:
Match each statement to a sign.

- **a** Put your rubbish in the bin.
- **b** Wait for the school bus here.
- **c** Don't smoke near the door.
- **d** Use the crossing.
- **e** You mustn't go there.
- **f** Look out for pumas.
- **g** You can't walk here at night.
- **h** Don't park here.

sign	1	2	3	4	5	6	7	8
statement								

Write the statements a–f using reported speech. Complete the following sentences. Look carefully at the tense of the introductory word, too.

- **a** Arthur told the boys ______________________
- **b** Fiona told her daughter ______________________
- **c** The hotel owner asked guests ______________________
- **d** The policemen advised the old people ______________________
- **e** The sign asks visitors ______________________
- **f** The national park warned people ______________________
- **g** Tom tells Peter ______________________
- **h** The Navajo Council orders people ______________________

Vocabulary

71 Learn some new words about cooking food. The English words are with an illustration – match these to the correct German words.

microwave – ______________

____

bake – ______________

grill – ______________

roast – ______________

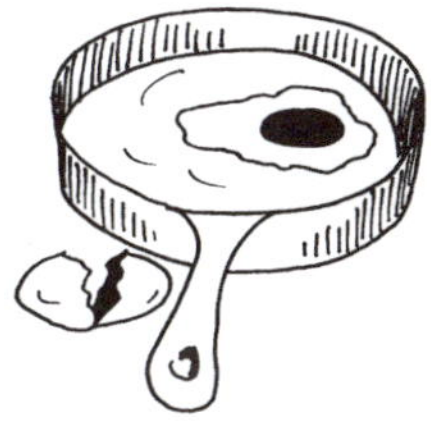

fry – ______________

boil – ______________

72 Look at the following pictures.
Explain how you, or people in your family, would cook each thing.

a My aunt would ____________________ a chicken.

b ____

c ____

d ____

e ____

f ____

g ____

Using your English

73 Explain how to make **toast Hawaii** or an **English breakfast** of eggs, bacon, sausages and toast.

Test

74 Write the following sentences as reported speech. Tip: underline the tense of the introductory verb before you start.

a *Bob:* "Have you bought a new car?"
Bob asked Julia ______________________________

____

b *Kim:* "This is my sister and she is staying with me until tomorrow."
Kim said ______________________________

____

c *Andrew:* "I'm looking for my coat because I've lost it."
Andrew explained ______________________________

____

d *Thomas:* "How do we make spaghetti bolognese?"
Thomas ______________________________

____

e *Carol:* "Last week we went to a nice restaurant."
Carol told Sue ______________________________

____

f *Jenny:* "Post the letter for me, please." *(asks, Mike)*

____

____

g *Linda:* "Don't swim in the cold river today." *(advised, the children)*

____

____

h *Mr and Mrs Fielder:* "We haven't visited our friends in America for a long time." *(explain, Jason)*

____

____

i *Sammy:* "Whose shoes are these?" *(wanted to know)*

____

____

Topic 10: What is Art?

Zita, Eric and Pippa are chatting on an internet site about a school trip.

Eric: "What's art?" – It's a good question. I have to write about that, too, after our trip.

Pippa: *Me, too. Did you go into that big box at that exhibition we saw at the Tate Modern in London?*

Eric: No, I didn't. Maybe Zita did.

Zita: *I didn't, either; what was it like? I had to go to Trafalgar Square because I have to write about the boat there.*

Eric: A boat in Trafalgar Square!

Zita: *It was an old boat – a galleon like those hundreds of year ago – and in a bottle. Maybe it had something to do with Trafalgar. That was a big sea battle more that 200 years ago, where Captain Nelson died – maybe he had a boat like the galleon. Pippa, tell me about the box.*

Pippa: *It was just a huge box – 13 metres high, 10 metres wide and 30 metres long. It was on 2-metre-high legs so you could walk under it. I didn't like that. I kept thinking it would fall on top of me! There was a ramp into the box but the inside was black.*

Eric: What do you mean – black?

Pippa: *I mean there was no light in it. It was black and scary. I walked into it, and you could hear lots of other people but you couldn't see them. I walked and walked and then came to the end wall.*

Zita: *Didn't people walk into each other?*

Pippa: *I wondered why that didn't happen but when I turned around you could see the light in the other direction. That meant you could see the people walking into the box and you just missed them when you walked out.*

Eric: Is that art?

Pippa: *Well, it was in an exhibition and in a very famous gallery. So it must be art.*

OK

Vocabulary

galleon: *Galeone (Segelschiff)*

Questions on the text

75 Are the statements *true, false* or *not in the text?*
Tick (✓) the correct box. Explain all your answers.

	true	false	not in the text
a The pupils have work to do after their visit. *True / False / Not in the text because* ________________ ________________	☐	☐	☐
b The exhibition was in Trafalgar Square. ________________ ________________	☐	☐	☐
c Nelson was a soldier at Trafalgar. ________________ ________________	☐	☐	☐
d Nelson's boat is very famous. ________________ ________________	☐	☐	☐
e Pippa expected the box to drop on her. ________________ ________________	☐	☐	☐
f Everyone could climb into the box. ________________ ________________	☐	☐	☐
g Pippa took a light with her. ________________ ________________	☐	☐	☐
h Pippa decided to explore the inside of the box. ________________ ________________	☐	☐	☐

i You could walk through the box. ☐ ☐ ☐

j There were a lot of accidents. ☐ ☐ ☐

76 Look at the photos. Which two things did the pupils see?

A ☐

B ☐

C ☐

D ☐

Grammar

Wann verwendest du den Infinitiv mit *to*?

- Der **Infinitiv mit *to*** steht **nach bestimmten Verben**, z. B. *(to) agree, can / be able to afford, attempt, choose, decide, expect, fail, hope, intend, learn, manage, offer, plan, promise, refuse, seem, try, want.*
  Beispiele: Pippa attempted to walk under the box.
  Eric decided not to write a lot.
- Der **Infinitiv mit *to* oder die *ing*-Form** können **nach bestimmten Verben** stehen, z. B. *(to) begin, continue, forget, hate, like, love, prefer, remember, start, stop* (siehe Seite 103).
  Beispiel: Zita starts to write / writing her story.

- Der **Infinitiv mit *to*** steht **nach bestimmten Verben + Objekt**, z. B. (to) *advise, allow, ask, cause, encourage, expect, force, help, invite, persuade, recommend, remind, teach, tell, want, warn, would like, would love.*
  Beispiele: She asked Peter to meet her.
  She asked Peter not to meet her.
- Der **Infinitiv mit *to*** kann eine **indirekte Frage mit einem modalen Hilfsverb** (z. B. *can, must, should*) **ersetzen.** Er steht nach Fragewörtern wie z. B. *who, what, where, when, which, how* und nach *whether.*
  Beispiel:

direct question	reported question
Joe: How can I get to the bus stop? *(Frage mit modalem Hilfsverb)*	Joe wanted to know how he could get to the bus stop. *(indirekte Frage)* Joe wanted to know how to get to the bus stop. (to + *Infinitiv*)

77 Complete the gaps with a question word and the word in brackets.

a Most people know ______________________ the internet. *(use)*

b Pippa explained ______________________ the information. *(find)*

c James asked her ______________________. *(phone)*

d Eric didn't know ______________________ in London. *(go)*

e The teacher told us ______________________. *(meet)*

f Do you know ______________________? *(paint)*

g Peter never knows ______________________ about. *(write)*

78 The pupils in the text wrote a page in their school magazine about their trip. They made a super layout which had small comments on pieces of paper all over the page. Complete what they wrote with the correct verb forms and using the *to*-infinitive where it is needed.

I wanted ______________ to the Tate Modern but my teacher told me ______________ to Trafalgar Square and ______________ about the art work there. I remembered ______________ my camera with me so I ______________ some interesting pictures. Zita, 9B2

I would love ______________ London again. I don't ______________ how people can afford ______________ there though. Everything ______________ really expensive. Our teacher warned us ______________ careful with our money there. He advised us ______________ our money in our back pockets of our jeans. We remembered ______________ that!

Eric, 9B2

It's easy to learn ______________ the Underground or the buses. I ______________ my way from one place to another with a street map. Some tourists even asked me ______________ them! It ______________ only because I ______________ a map.

Pippa 9B2

- Mit ***used* + *to* + Infinitiv** beziehst du dich auf die **Vergangenheit**. Du drückst aus,
  - dass eine **Handlung regelmäßig** stattfand oder
  - dass ein **Zustand** vorherrschte.

  Du betonst dadurch, dass dies in der Gegenwart nicht mehr der Fall ist.
  Beispiel: I used to live in London but I live here now. *Früher lebte ich in London …*

  Verwechsle *used* + *to* + Infinitiv nicht mit *(to) be used to* + *ing*-Form (= gewöhnt sein, etwas zu tun) oder *(to) be used to something* (= an etwas gewöhnt sein).
  Beispiele: Jenny used to fly frequently. = She doesn't fly anymore.
  (Früher flog Jenny häufig.)
  Jenny is used to flying. = She often flies and has no problems with it.
  (Jenny ist an das Fliegen gewöhnt.)

79 Read the sentences carefully.
Do you need *used to* or *(to) be used to* to complete them? Tick (✓) the correct box and complete the sentence with the verb in the right form.

a Eric's grandad … a painter.

☐ used to ______________ *(be)*

☐ is used to ______________ *(be)*

b The 9th class … interesting projects; they have done many of them already.

- ☐ used to ______________ *(do)*
- ☐ are used to ______________ *(do)*

c Pippa … lots of photographs but she has now stopped.

- ☐ used to ______________ *(take)*
- ☐ is used to ______________ *(take)*

d Mr and Mrs Johnson … on the floor – their backs hurt.

- ☐ used to ______________ *(work)*
- ☐ aren't used to ______________ *(work)*

e Michael and Johnny … to school but now they go by bus.

- ☐ used to ______________ *(cycle)*
- ☐ are used to ______________ *(cycle)*

f Steffie … the piano at the school fair but this year she is helping us.

- ☐ used to ______________ *(play)*
- ☐ is used to ______________ *(play)*

g The school fair … on a Saturday.

- ☐ used to ______________ *(be)*
- ☐ was used to ______________ *(be)*

h Everyone … a fun time at the school fair in the summer.

- ☐ used to ______________ *(have)*
- ☐ is used to ______________ *(have)*

i After the project everyone has to help to tidy up but they … that.

- ☐ used to
- ☐ are used to

j Gina complained of a bad back; she … the hard work!

- ☐ used to
- ☐ isn't used to

- Der Infinitiv mit *to* kann einen **Relativsatz ersetzen**. Er steht dann **nach einem Nomen**, den Pronomen ***anything*** und ***something*** sowie nach **Mengenangaben** wie *a lot of, lots of, much, many*.
  Beispiele: The path that they should use is over there.
  → The path to use is over there.
  Have you got anything that I could read?
  → Have you got anything to read?
  There are lots of windows that have to be washed.
  → There are lots of windows to wash.
- Der Infinitiv mit *to* kann **nach** den meisten **Adjektiven und ihren Steigerungsformen** sowie **nach *too*** und ***enough*** in Verbindung mit einem Adjektiv stehen.
  Beispiele: It is faster to walk.
  It is too late to phone.
  John's car is not big enough to carry all his friends.

80 The year 9 pupils wanted to do an art project at their summer fair *(Schulfest)*. They decided to wrap up a classroom like the famous artist Christo and get everyone to help – parents, teachers and other visitors. They made some signs and the visitors talked a lot while they were helping. Complete the signs and the comments people made.

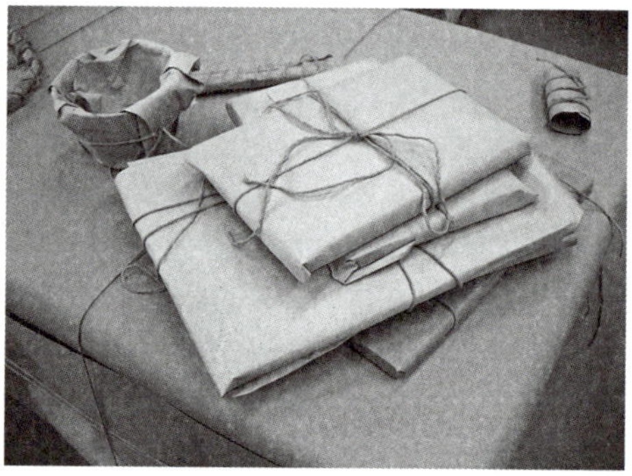

a The paper ______________________ *(nutzen)* is here.

b If you want something ____________________________ *(schneiden)* the paper with, it's on the table.

c The string ___________________ *(binden)* things with is next to the scissors.

d There is a lot of work ______________________ *(tun)*, so please help.

e The objects _________________________ *(einpacken)* are on the tables but we have to start with the walls and the floor.

f We have put the information __________________________ *(lesen)* about the project on the door.

g The chair is too difficult for me ____________________________ *(einpacken)*.

h My fingers are too big ____________________ *(zubinden)* the string.

i Have you got enough paper ______________ *(bedecken)* the whole room?

j It's easier ____________________ *(anfangen)* with the legs of the table.

k The hardest thing ______________________ *(tun)* was the blackboard.

Vocabulary

81 Trafalgar Square is often used for art work. One artist did something unusual there. Read the original sign on the left; then look at the sign on the right which has some synonyms in it to help you understand it. Answer the questions about the words in full sentences.

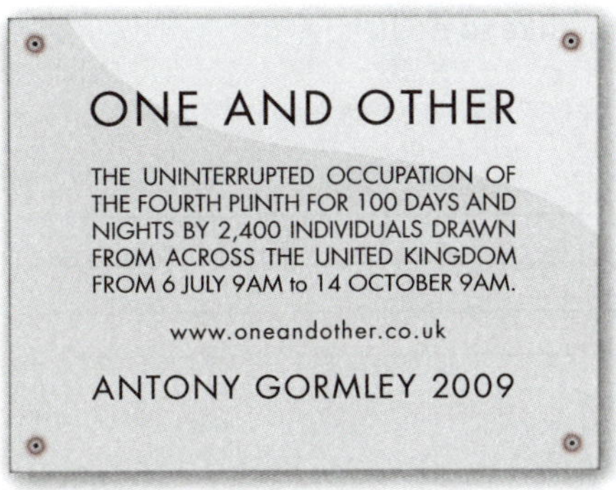

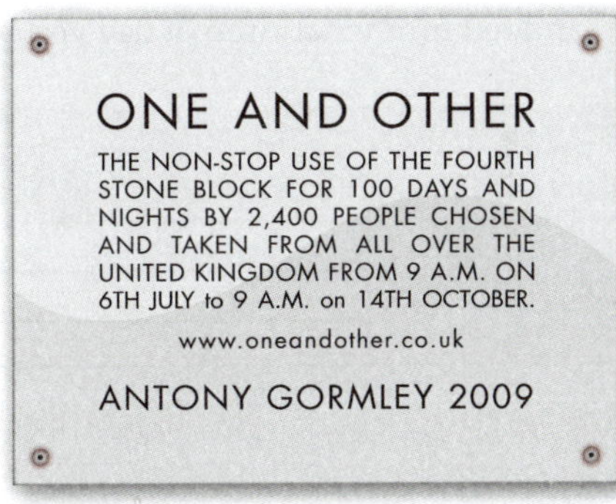

a What does "uninterrupted" mean? Think of a German word for this, too.

____

b Explain what these words mean in German or give the German equivalent *(Entsprechung)*.

- (the) use ______________________________
- (to) use ______________________________
- used to ______________________________
- (to) be used to ______________________________

c What is the correct word for the object a sculpture or work of art stands on?

____

d What is the title of the art work and who "made" it?

____

e Give a synonym for a.m.

____

f How long did each person stand in Trafalgar Square?

____

Using your English

82 Imagine that the artist wanted people from all over the world to stand on the plinth. E-mail him and ask to be part of the art work in Trafalgar Square.
In your e-mail …

- explain why you want to do this,
- say what you would do while you were on top of it,
- and tell him what time of day you would like to do it.

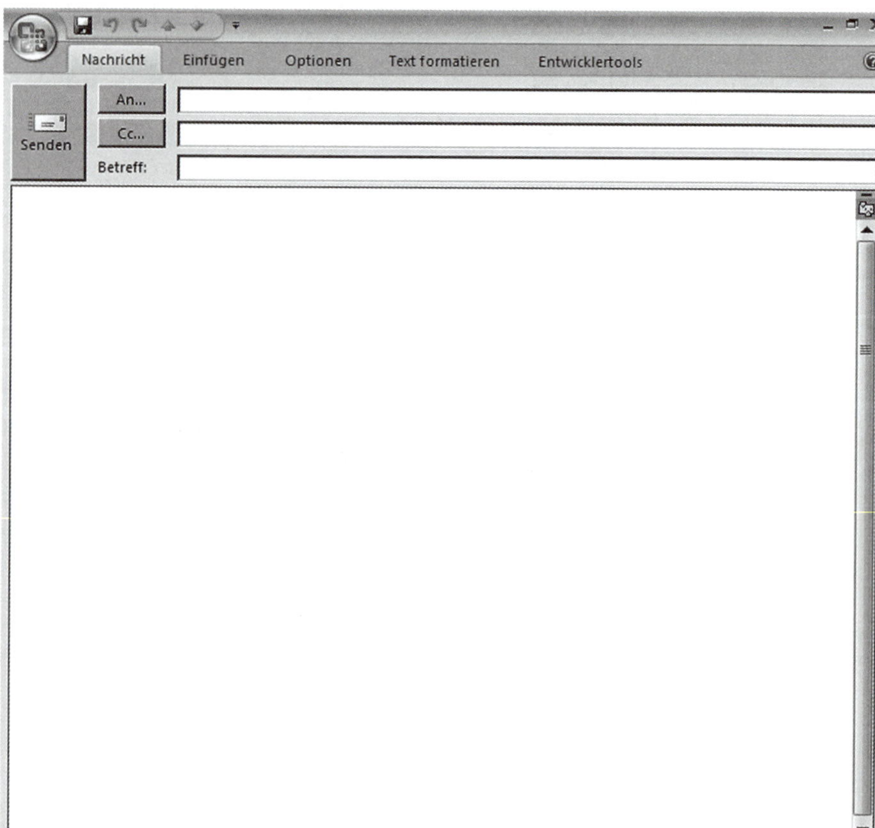

Test

83 Complete the gaps.

a Do you know where ______________ Mike a present? *(buy)*

b I don't know who ______________ about my car. *(phone)*

c Is there anything interesting ______________ in London? *(see)*

d Linda would like ______________ Manchester. *(visit)*

e Is it quicker ______________? *(drive)*

f Can I ask John ______________ me tomorrow? *(help)*

g Sally asked Mike how ______________ her bike. *(repair)*

84 Be careful, not every sentence needs the *to*-infinitive this time.

a Sally says it's too early ______________ swimming. *(go)*

b Harry can't afford ______________ to New York. *(fly)*

c Mum's car ______________ dirtier and dirtier every day. *(get)*

d The T-shirt ______________ is the red one. *(buy)*

e I would have ______________ nicer weather. *(expect)*

f I would love ______________ a dog. *(have)*

g Sally expected ______________ the race. *(not/win)*

h The journey ___________ longer than I ______________ it. *(be/remember)*

i Larry's garden was big enough ______________ football in. *(play)*

j I had hoped ____________ French when I ___________ to Paris. *(learn/go)*

k We remembered ____________ all the windows before we left. *(close)*

l The boys were told ____________ on the grass. *(not/walk)*

m Anna ______________ to work but she prefers ______________ there. *(drive/cycle)*

n The man ______________ the door and then began ____________ his book. *(close/read)*

o Jason wanted to know how ______________ the carpet dirty when he ______________ the wall. *(not/get/paint)*

Topic 11: The Grand Canyon

A You cannot avoid being impressed by the Grand Canyon. It is much larger than you expect it to be. The canyon is 446 kilometres long and on average it is 16 kilometres wide in a straight line from side to side. The canyon is 2,438 metres above sea level, which means the air is thin and you have to move slowly and drink more water. From the top to the bottom it is 1,524 metres, or more than 1.5 kilometres.

B Lying at the bottom of the canyon is the Colorado River. At 2,333 kilometres long, it's one of America's longest rivers. It begins in the Rocky Mountains and meets the sea just across the border of Mexico on the west coast. During its time in the Grand Canyon the Colorado River is usually about 11 metres deep but in places it reaches 30 metres.

C Until 1869 no one had travelled through the Grand Canyon. John Wesley Powell wanted to explore the Colorado River and set off on a three-month journey by boat which took him into the canyon. There were no maps for him to follow so he never knew what was around the next corner of the river. The boats he used were simple but strong but some were still destroyed. Losing boats, food and equipment was bad news but in the middle of the canyon three of his men didn't want to go on. They decided to leave the group and started walking home; they were never seen again. Powell continued his journey by boat and 98 days after he had begun it, 24 of them in the Grand Canyon itself, he and his small group of men came out of the western end of it alive.

D There are walks in the Grand Canyon but walking to the river and back is not possible in one day. Walking uphill there takes twice as long as walking downhill. So a two-hour walk down is a four-hour walk back. There is no shade in the canyon and temperatures are often 16 ° warmer at the bottom of the canyon than at the top of it. For every hour you walk you must drink one litre of water. You shouldn't walk between 10 a.m. and 4 p.m. because of the heat.

Vocabulary

impressed (paragraph A): *beeindruckt*
sea level (paragraph A): *Meeresspiegel*
(to) set off (paragraph C): *aufbrechen*
alive (paragraph C): *lebendig*

Questions on the text

85 Give each paragraph a heading. There are two headings which are not needed. Write the correct heading next to the paragraph it belongs to.

Exploring the river
River facts
CANYON HISTORY
?
Looking after yourself
Boat trips
No small place

Paragraph	Heading
A	
B	
C	
D	

86 Label *(beschriften)* the two diagrams.

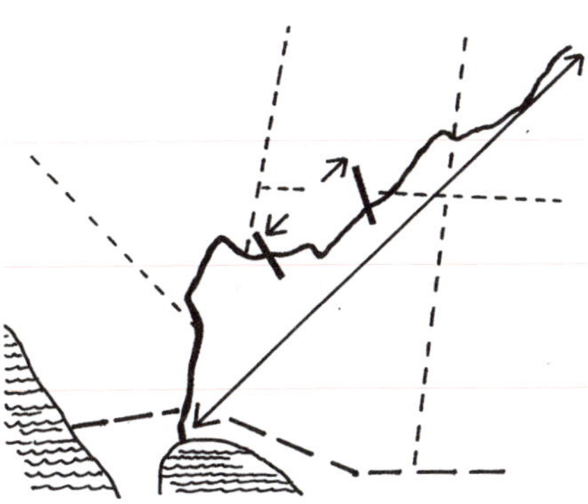

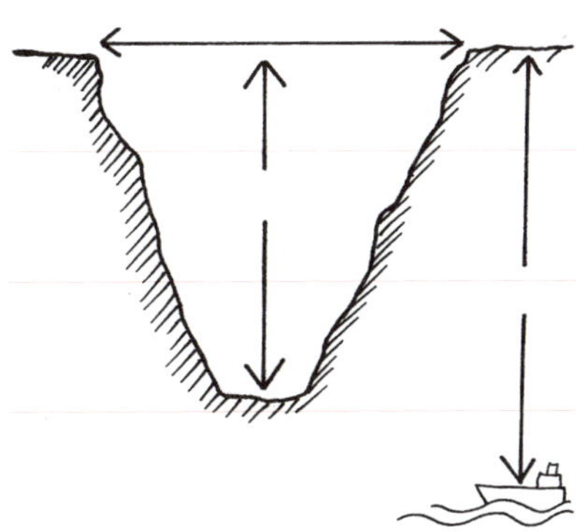

87 Read the text again carefully and answer the following questions in 1–5 words or numbers, where possible.

a Why is it necessary to walk slowly and to drink a lot?

____

b What made the river dangerous for Powell and his group?

____

c How long were Powell and his men in the Grand Canyon itself?

____

d If it takes you twelve hours to walk to the top of the rim from the river, how long did it take you to go down?

____

e If you walked for four hours, how much water should you drink?

____

f When should you walk?

____

Grammar

Welche Funktionen kann die *-ing*-Form im Satz übernehmen?

Mit der ***-ing*-Form** wird die **Verlaufsform von Verben** gebildet.
Beispiel: He is eating an ice cream.

Die ***-ing*-Form** kann aber auch **andere Funktionen im Satz** übernehmen. Sie wird dann wie ein **Nomen** verwendet.

- Die ***-ing*-Form** kann **Subjekt** des Satzes sein.
  Beispiel: Reading is something I do in the evening.
- **Nach bestimmten Verben** kann die ***-ing*-Form** als **Objekt** des Satzes verwendet werden, z. B. nach *(to) admit, avoid, can't stand, consider, dislike, enjoy, fancy, finish, give up, go on, imagine, keep, (don't) mind, mention, miss, practise, risk, suggest.*
  Beispiel: They finished reading on the train.
- Die ***-ing*-Form** kann **nach** einer **Präposition** oder **Konjunktion der Zeit** stehen (siehe Seite 102).
  Beispiel: After visiting the Grand Canyon we went to Las Vegas.

Beachte: Die *-ing*-Form kann auch eine **Ergänzung** bei sich haben.
Beispiel: Reading books is something I do in the evening.

88 Look at the illustrations and then complete the gaps in the sentences with a suitable verb.

- **a** I can't imagine ______________________ in that house over there.
- **b** ______________________ is allowed in the Grand Canyon National Park.
- **c** ______________________ when it is hot is dangerous.
- **d** Most old people can only stand ______________________ in the sunshine a short time.
- **e** ______________________ through the Grand Canyon is possible.
- **f** ______________________ the animals is not allowed.
- **g** Many people enjoy ______________________ in the restaurant.
- **h** I suggest ______________________ for the bus here.
- **i** We enjoyed ______________________ at the view.

In welchen Fällen steht die *-ing*-Form nach einer Präposition oder Konjunktion?

Die *-ing*-**Form** steht **nach**:

- einem **Adjektiv + Präposition**:
  z. B.: *(to be) interested in, (to be) tired of, (to be) afraid of, (to be) good at.*
  Beispiel: I am afraid of walking alone in the dark.
- einem **Verb + Präposition**:
  z. B.: *(to) talk about, (to) think of, (to) complain of/about, (to) look forward to.*
  Beispiel: She is thinking of buying a new car.
- einem **Nomen + Präposition**:
  z. B.: *(the) chance of, (the) danger of, (the) interest in, (the) reason for.*
  Beispiel: You have the chance of winning the competition.
- einer **Präposition**:
  z. B.: *instead of, in spite of.*
  Beispiel: Instead of driving to London she went by train.
- einer **Konjunktion der Zeit**:
  z. B. *while, when, since.*
  Beispiel: While swimming she hurt her foot.
- **folgenden Ausdrücken**:
  (to) be no use, (to) be worth, What about …?, How about …?
  Beispiel: What about phoning Tom tonight?

89 Complete the sentences using the correct verb forms. Some sentences do not use the *-ing*-form.

a I apologise for ________________ late. *(be)*

b Before ________________ the house I ________________ the newspaper. *(leave/read)*

c Yesterday I ________________ to the cinema. *(drive)*

d Instead of ________________ I ________________ by bus last night. *(cycle/go)*

e I ________________ some e-mails while ________________ on the train. *(write/travel)*

f Do you often ________________ in the park? *(jog)*

g Do you worry about ________________ where there ________________ snakes? *(walk/be)*

h It's not worth ________________ Toni tonight; she ________________ at a party. *(phone/be)* i After ________________ the Grand Canyon we ________________ in Las Vegas. *(visit/stay)*

j Charlie said he would ________________ to Sam after ________________ to Amanda. *(speak/talk)*

Wann verwendest du die -*ing*-Form und wann den Infinitiv?

- Nach bestimmten Verben kannst du die -*ing*-**Form** oder den **Infinitiv mit *to* ohne Bedeutungsunterschied** verwenden.
  Häufig verwendete Verben sind: *(to) begin, continue, hate, like, love, prefer* und *start*.
  Beispiel: We began walking at 7.00 a.m.
  We began to walk at 7.00 a.m.
  Beachte: Nach *would like, would hate, would love* und *would prefer* **muss** der Infinitiv stehen.
  Beispiel: I would prefer to stay in that hotel.
- Nach den Verben ***(to) stop, forget*** und ***remember*** kannst du auch die **-*ing*-Form** oder den **Infinitiv mit *to*** verwenden. Allerdings **ändert sich** hier die **Bedeutung**.

Beispiele:	We stopped buying chocolate.	=	We don't buy chocolate any more.
	We stopped to buy chocolate.	=	We stopped and then bought chocolate.
	I forgot to read the book.	=	I didn't read the book.
	I forgot reading the book.	=	I had read the book but couldn't remember doing that.
	She remembered to phone me.	=	She phoned me sometime later.
	She remembered phoning me.	=	She has already phoned and could remember that she did this.

90 Complete the sentences with the correct verb forms. Where there are two possible answers, you only need to give one.

a The bus driver continued ________________ along the road. *(drive)*

b I would like ________________ the Grand Canyon. *(visit)*

c Pam would prefer ________________ to New York. *(fly)*

d We loved ________________ the fantastic views. *(look at)*

e We have just begun ________________ the car. *(wash)*

f They hated ________________ a long way. *(travel)*

g She would love ________________ the film. *(watch)*

91 What do the following sentences mean? Tick (✓) the correct box.

a Paula remembered to send Zoe an e-mail.

☐ Paula did not forget to send Zoe an e-mail.
☐ Paula can remember that she sent Zoe an e-mail.

b George remembers flying to America.

☐ George has to fly to America.
☐ George can remember when he flew to America.

c We stopped buying newspapers a few weeks ago.

☐ We have not bought any newspapers for a few weeks now.
☐ A few weeks ago we bought some newspapers.

d Tom stopped to look into a shop's window.

☐ Tom used to look into a shop's window but he now doesn't.
☐ Tom stopped and then looked into a shop's window.

e Lucy always forgets to take her camera with her.

☐ Lucy can never remember that she has got her camera with her.
☐ Lucy's camera is at home.

f I forgot buying this T-shirt.

☐ I should have bought the T-shirt but I didn't.
☐ I have just found this T-shirt that I had bought.

g They remember to meet Larry at the hotel.

☐ They have met Larry before and can remember him.
☐ They haven't forgotten that they will meet Larry.

h She stopped e-mailing Mike years ago.

☐ She often e-mailed Mike a long time ago but doesn't any more.
☐ When she was e-mailing Mike, she had to stop.

92 Read the sign which is on the Grand Canyon bus. You will see that there are eight statements on it. Complete the sentences about the statements.

GRAND CANYON – **Summer Hiking**

DON'T SUFFER. HIKE SMART!

- Drink plenty of water and electrolyte drinks.
- Eat carbohydrates and salty foods.
- Hike during the cooler parts of the day. (before 10 a.m., after 4 p.m.)
- Go slowly and rest often.
- Get wet to stay cool.

GRAND · CANYON HIKE SMART

The National Park Service does not recommend hiking to the river and back in one day!

Vocabulary
electrolyte drinks: *mineralhaltige Getränke*
carbohydrates: *Kohlenhydrate*

a ______________________ in summer in the Grand Canyon

b Instead of __________________ hike smart.

c When walking a long way start ______________________________ and electrolyte drinks.

d ______________________________ and __________________ is necessary.

e Remember ____

f ______________________ and ______________________ can save your life.

g Don't forget ____

h The National Park would prefer people not __________________________

____

Vocabulary

93 Word building: Look at the three lists. Select a word, a prefix or a suffix from the second list and use it correctly with a word in the first. Write the new English word and match it to its German meaning.

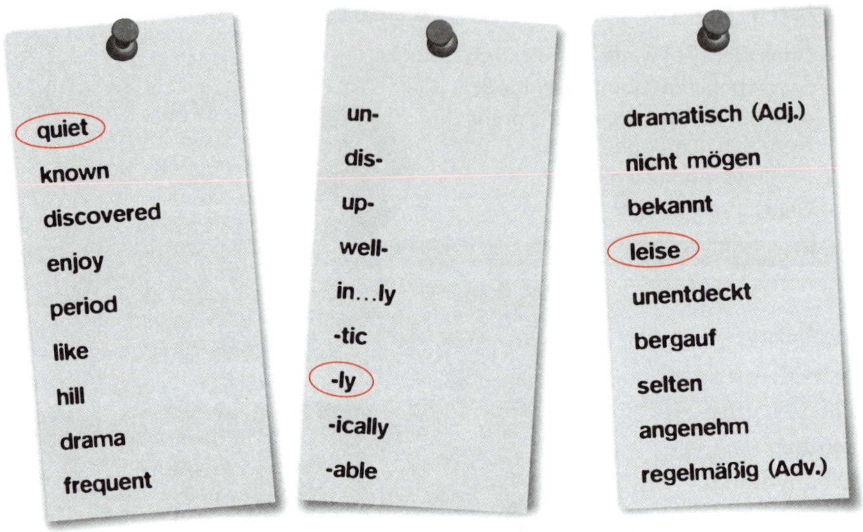

English word	in German
quietly	*leise*

94 Imagine that you visited the Grand Canyon and had to write a small report about it. Fill in the missing words using the new vocabulary from exercise 93.

Today the Grand Canyon is a very ______________ place but it was ______________ for a very long time. ______________ there are thunderstorms which can be very ______________ over the canyon. Most animals ______________ people but if you walk ______________ along the paths in the National Park you will probably see a lot of them. Tourists find it very ______________ to take photos of the deer and the other wildlife that they meet. There are snakes and mountain lions, too, but these are ______________ seen.
What is also nice about the Grand Canyon National Park is that most paths there are very flat so you seldom have difficult ______________ walks to make unless you go to the bottom of the canyon.

Using your English

95 You and your family have been visiting the Grand Canyon. Write an e-mail to your American e-pal telling him or her about it.

- Write at least two sentences about each photo in order (1–4).
- Explain to your friend where you were, what was there, and what you did, for example, so that you make a short report for your friend.

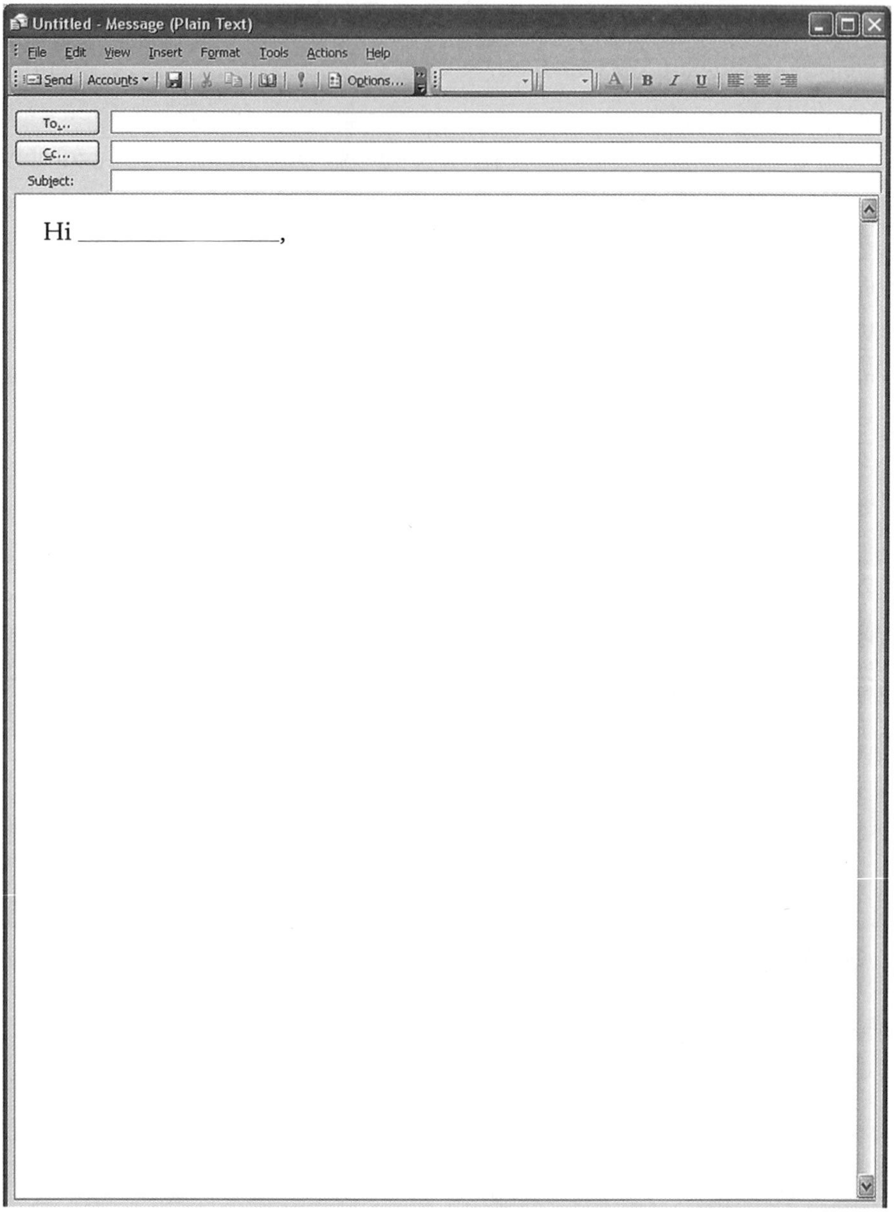

96 A new face on the South Rim

A new face on the South Rim

The Grand Canyon has some new inhabitants – cougars. Cougars are not often seen but they are on the South Rim. We want everyone to enjoy their stay in the National Park – people and animals. For that reason we would like you to take care when walking along the paths and through the forest.

Here are some simple rules:
- Don't walk alone, always stay in groups and walk noisily.
- Make sure that your children are not far away from you and you can see them.
- Never leave food where an animal can find it.

We don't want to scare our visitors but if you meet a cougar and it doesn't move away, you should try the following tactics:
- Never run away from one, instead walk slowly backwards away from it.
- Make yourself big – for example, put you arms above your head.
- The louder you are, the better.
- Don't allow anyone to leave your group – so keep together.

There are very few cougars in the area, so please tell a ranger if you see one.

You have just read about the cougars in a guide book and are talking to your friend in German. Suddenly someone starts talking to you in German, too. Can you give the person the information she asks for?

Frau: Entschuldigung, kannst du mir helfen? Ich habe ein Schild über Berglöwen gesehen. Gibt es hier wirklich welche? Ist die Wahrscheinlichkeit groß, dass mir einer über den Weg läuft?

Du: ______________________________

Frau: Die Tiere sind doch bestimmt gefährlich. Warum verjagen die Ranger sie nicht?

Du: ______________________________

Frau: Ich wollte heute spazieren gehen. Gibt es dafür Ratschläge?

Du: ______________________________

____

____

____

____

Frau: Aber wie soll ich mich verhalten, wenn ich dennoch auf einen Berglöwen treffe?

Du: ______________________________

____

____

____

Frau: Sollte ich irgendetwas machen, nachdem ich einen Berglöwen gesehen habe?

Du: ______________________________

Frau: Warum?

Du: ______________________________

Frau: Vielen Dank für deine Hilfe.

Test

97 Complete the sentences with the correct verb forms.
Be careful, some sentences have nothing to do with *-ing*-forms.

a I forgot ______________ Jane a birthday card. She will ______________ angry with me. *(buy/be)*

b Rob is afraid of ______________ on a snake. I would prefer not ______________ one, either. *(stand/meet)*

c I hated ______________ as a child. *(swim)*

d ______________ in cars ______________ me tired. *(travel/make)*

e Nina ______________ quietly through the forest yesterday. *(walk)*

f I would like ______________ a fast car. *(own)*

g ______________ isn't a sport I like. *(fish)*

h How about ______________ with us tonight? *(stay)*

i I want ______________ instead of ______________ TV. *(read/watch)*

j We ______________ from the national park. We ______________ a great time there. *(just return/have)*

k After ______________ the door, she ______________ her key. *(close/lose)*

l It will be no use ______________ Eva tonight, she ______________ to America. *(phone/fly)*

m Harry ______________ to Jane before he ______________ on holiday. *(speak/go)*

n I fancy ______________ some new clothes tomorrow. *(buy)*

o We ______________ together a lot while ______________. *(talk/jog)*

Topic 12: Need something done?

ComputerDoc

Computer system not working?

- Phone us, the experts!
- 24hr-a-day home service
- No problem too large or too small
- Good prices
- Software installations

www.compdoc.com
Mobile tel.: 0459722354
ComputerDoc, 12 Low Street, Darlington

Rosie's Interiors

Decorating ideas?
Painting needing doing
Curtain and furniture ideas
Rosie's Interiors help
with any problem
inside your house.
Good advice – good service.

Open: 9 a.m. – 5.30 p.m. Mon – Sat
Tel: 0354 / 22884
Rosie's Interiors, New Road, Croft

Castle Beauty Centre

Look good – feel good.
Come along to our centre for a free talk.
See what we can do for you – men, too.
Hair, nails, skin –
after we have finished with you,
you won't know yourself in the mirror.

Appointments: Tel. 0567/1121
www.cbc.com
Castle Beauty Centre, 4 The Market Place, Richmond

SAM'S GARAGE

- Repairs of all kinds
- Sound systems fitted
- Tuning, spraying, cleaning
- Something different – something cool?

Sam's Garage, 24 Bridge Street, Hurworth
Tel: 0456/44228 · www.samsgarage.com

Questions on the text

98 Answer the questions about the adverts.
You do not have to write full sentences.

a Who will come to your house in the middle of the night?

____

b Freddie has just damaged his father's car. Where should he go before he goes home?

____

c Mr and Mrs Silver have just moved into an old house and it's horrible. Who do they go to?

____

d Henriette wants wide wheels on her car. Which telephone number does she phone?

____

e Where can you get advice for no money?

____

f Which company's prices are probably OK?

____

g Mike is going to a wedding at the weekend and wants to look good. Which website does he go to?

____

h Jason is having the outside of his house painted but he needs some ideas for his living room, too. Who helps him?

____

i Emma loves technology. Who does she phone to see if she can get a Saturday job?

____

j Bob has already found a job. He enjoys listening to music and doing different things. Where does he work?

____

Grammar

Wann verwendest du *have something done*?

Du verwendest *have + Objekt + past participle*, um zu erklären, **was jemand von einer anderen Person machen lässt / ließ / lassen wird**.

Beispiele: Sam has his photo taken.
Elle is having her car washed.
They had their car cleaned.

Beachte den Unterschied zum *present perfect:*

Beispiel:	Harry has painted his front door.	present perfect: *Harry hat seine Haustür gestrichen.*
	Harry has his front door painted.	have + *Objekt* + past participle: *Harry lässt seine Haustür streichen.* → *Eine andere Person streicht Harrys Tür.*
	Harry has had his front door painted.	have + *Objekt* + past participle *im* present perfect: *Harry hat seine Haustür streichen lassen.*

99 What is being done by other people? The illustrations will give you the answers. Use a form of *have + object + past participle* in your sentences.

a Jane never wanted a white car.

Jane ____________________ her car ________________.

b Harry hates his long hair.

Harry ____________________ his long hair ____________.

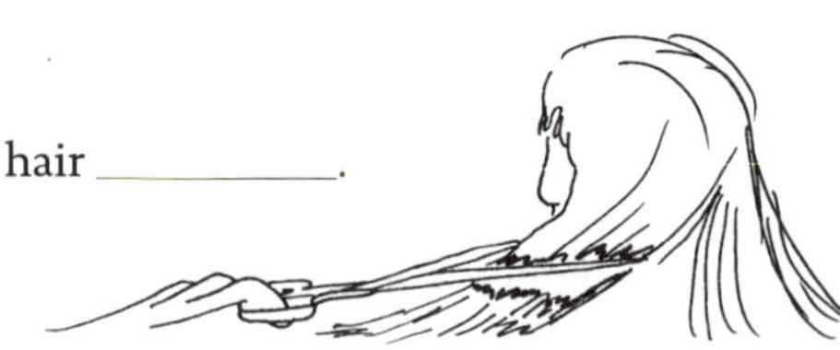

c Tom's computer broke down yesterday.

____

____

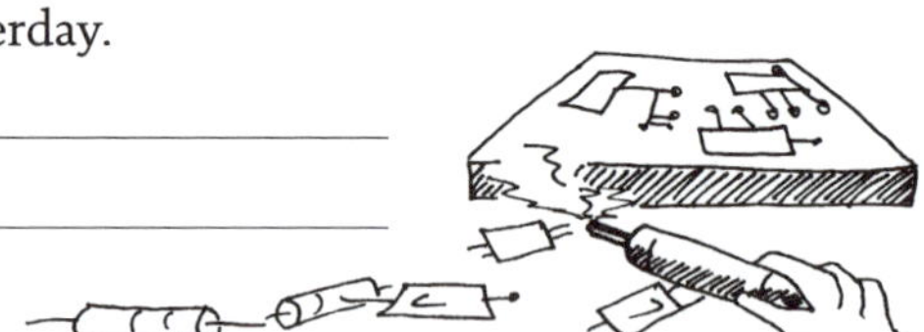

d Mrs Flower's curtains don't fit the windows in her new house.

____

____

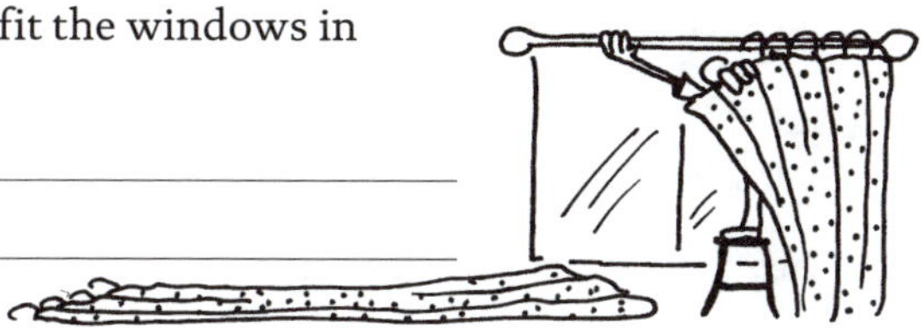

e I dropped some paint on my carpet – it needs cleaning.

____

____

f They want to change their sofa.

____

____

100 Read the sentences carefully. Then tick (✓) the correct meaning.

a Anne is having her coat repaired.

☐ Someone is repairing the coat for Anne.

☐ Anne is repairing her coat herself.

b Trevor has driven to Newcastle.

☐ Someone has driven Trevor to Newcastle.

☐ Trevor drove to Newcastle himself.

c Ronnie has sent an e-mail.

☐ Someone has sent Ronnie an e-mail.

☐ Ronnie has sent the e-mail himself.

d Kathy has an e-mail sent.

☐ Someone sent the e-mail for Kathy.

☐ Kathy sent the e-mail herself.

e We have our hotel room cleaned.
- ☐ Someone is cleaning the hotel room.
- ☐ We cleaned the hotel room ourselves.

f They have taken some photos.
- ☐ Someone has taken the photos of the other people.
- ☐ The people have taken the photos themselves.

g The tourists have had maps given.
- ☐ Someone has given the tourists the maps.
- ☐ The tourists have bought the maps themselves.

h Michael has bought a map.
- ☐ Someone has bought a map for Michael.
- ☐ Michael bought the map himself.

i The man had his garden hut built.
- ☐ Someone built the garden hut for the man.
- ☐ The man had built the garden hut alone.

j The woman has designed the logo.
- ☐ Someone has designed the logo for the woman.
- ☐ The woman has designed the logo herself.

Vocabulary

101 When you answer an advert, there are some phrases that you often use. Here are some to learn.

- My name is …
- I'm phoning / writing about (your advert).
  I saw your advert … in the newspaper / a magazine / on TV / on the internet.
- I visited your website and …
  - I would like …
  - I'm interested in …
  - I would like to know …
- Would it be possible …?
- I'm looking forward to hearing from you,
- Kind regards,

Using your English

102 Imagine that your computer has a virus and you can't repair it. Contact the company at the start of this chapter which can help you. You leave a message on the answer phone. Write what you would say. Some tips about what to write are given below.

Sage deinen Namen.
Erkläre, woher du von der Firma weißt.
Erkläre das Problem.
Frage, ob sie dich anrufen können – wann und wo?

103 Luke was going to meet Anna from Germany tonight but something has happened. Their friend Marie is having to translate for them both. Complete the missing parts of the dialogue. You need to write in German when someone's name is underlined.

Luke: Hello Marie. Can you tell Anna that I can't meet her tonight. I'm having my car repaired.

Marie: That's no problem. Anna, ______

Anna: Oje! Was lässt er machen?

Marie: Ich frage ihn. Luke, ______

Luke: I'm having a new door put on it. Someone has damaged one of them and I can't close it.

Marie: Er sagt, dass ______________________________

____

____

Test

104 Read each sentence carefully. From the information given write a new sentence using the *have something done* construction.

a A man is taking Linda's photo.

Linda _is having_ her photo _taken._

b The doctor is testing Tony's eyes.

Tony ______________ his eyes ______________

c The woman at the beauty centre is painting the girls' nails.

____

d The bike shop repaired Sam's bike.

____

e If you want a new haircut, you can go to "Hair&Style".

You ______________________________

f Mr Jones decorated my parents' living room.

____

g The shop will make them their shoes.

____

h Tina looks after Sheila and Bruce's dogs when they go out.

____

i Simon cooks their meals for them.

____

Topic 13: Drop, cover, hold on

"Drop, cover, hold on" are four words which could save your life in California. California is an area where earthquakes can happen. In fact, most people expect a large earthquake in San Francisco or Los Angeles at some time during the next fifty years. The last large ones were in San Francisco in 1989 and in Los Angeles in 1994.

People living in California have read about what they should do in an earthquake but visitors, of course, haven't. During a strong earthquake the floor of a building moves very quickly, glass flies through the air and many other things, too. Although photos of earthquakes usually show many buildings which have collapsed, most buildings in California won't do this because they have been built for earthquakes.

What you do in the first few seconds of a strong earthquake can save your life. As soon as one starts, drop onto the floor and crawl to find shelter. Some people don't do this and are then badly injured.

Most injuries are from flying and falling objects so finding shelter is important. It is best to go under a strong table or desk and hold on to it – you must hold on to it to stop it moving away from you. If you cannot reach shelter in a few seconds, sit near an inside wall or next to low furniture, curl up into a ball and put your hands over your head and neck to protect them.

What you mustn't do during an earthquake in California is go outside or stay near outside walls – walls can collapse and glass windows can easily break. You also shouldn't sit under a door entrance – it can fall down – and it doesn't protect you from flying objects.

Finally, you should stay inside until the earthquake stops. Remember that after it there may be no electricity, water on the floor, damaged stairs and other dangers but never use the lift to get out of a building.

Vocabulary

earthquake (line 2): *Erdbeben*
shelter (line 13): *Schutz*
furniture (line 18): *Möbel*
(to) curl up (line 18):
sich zusammenrollen

A collapsed house in the San Francisco area after the earthquake of 1989

Questions on the text

105 Are the statements *true*, *false* or *not in the text?*
Tick (✓) the correct box.

	true	false	not in the text
a The advice is for everyone living in earthquake areas.	☐	☐	☐
b The worst earthquake was more than 100 years ago.	☐	☐	☐
c Tourists usually don't know what to do in an earth-quake.	☐	☐	☐
d Buildings in California shouldn't be badly damaged by an earthquake.	☐	☐	☐
e If the earthquake doesn't stop quickly, find some shelter.	☐	☐	☐
f You should lie down on the floor during the earth-quake.	☐	☐	☐
g If you are outside, stay far away from buildings.	☐	☐	☐
h It is a good idea to be next to an outside wall.	☐	☐	☐
i The police and firemen will look for people after an earthquake.	☐	☐	☐
j When the earthquake has stopped, the danger has gone.	☐	☐	☐

106 Explain why you ticked any *false* answers in exercise 105.

___

___

___

___

___

___

___

___

___

107 Look at the nine illustrations. Tick (✓) the ones which are true.

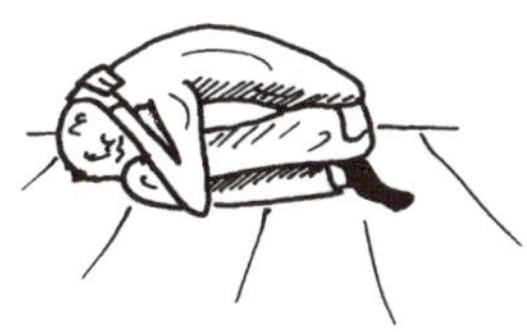

Grammar

Wann verwendest du ein modales Hilfsverb + *have* + *past participle*?

Du verwendest ein modales Hilfsverb (z. B. *could / should / would*) + *have* + *past participle*, wenn du sagen willst, was du in der **Vergangenheit** in einer Situation **getan haben könntest, solltest** oder **getan hättest.**

Beispiele: They could have gone to the cinema.
He should have phoned Mike.
I would have painted the boat yellow.

108 What *could, should* or *would have happened* in the following situations? If there is more than one answer possible, give the one you think is the best.

a It wasn't raining, so the boys ______________________________ football outside. *(play)*

b Julie ______________________________ if she had more money. *(fly)*

c I ______________________________ an earlier bus but I didn't. *(catch)*

d Tom doesn't think he ______________________________ so much at lunch-time – he's got stomach ache now. *(eat)*

e Sally ______________________________ a doctor but she wanted to be a teacher. *(become)*

f The girls ______________________________ to the cinema but they went to the theatre instead. *(go)*

g We ______________________________ at the weather forecast before we went to the beach – it rained! *(look at)*

h They ______________________________ sandwiches with them but they didn't have enough bread. *(take)*

109 Read the text again carefully.

- Complete the sentences using *could/should/would + have + past participle.*
- Some sentences use the negative forms – *couldn't, shouldn't* or *wouldn't.*
- The verbs to use are in the box but are not in the correct order.

find – think – hold on – sit – read – save

a These four words ______________________________ many lives in the past.

b Anybody living in California ______________________________ about what to do in an earthquake.

c But most visitors ______________________________ about earthquakes before they arrive.

d Many people ______________________________ shelter under tables but there weren't any in the room.

e The man went under the table but he ______________________________ to it.

f The people who were hurt ______________________________ next to the outside wall.

Vocabulary

110 **a** Verbs and nouns: Complete the gaps in the list.

verb	noun
(to) injure	
	protection
	rescue
(to) shelter	
	survival
(to) warn	

b To which group of words can you add a person? This is not possible with every group of words so think carefully.
For example: (to) report – report – **reporter**

____

____

Using your English

111 Imagine that you have to design an easy to understand earthquake awareness poster for a hotel room. Remember you need a good heading and only the most important information is necessary – you may use some simple diagrams, too.

Test

112 Complete the following sentences using *could/should/would + have + past participle*. The verb you need for each sentence is in the brackets.

a We ______________________ in Los Angeles; it wasn't very nice. *(not stay)*

b Rebecca ______________________ her bike faster but she didn't. *(ride)*

c The lorry driver ______________________ over the bridge – it was too small for it. *(not drive)*

d The pilot ______________________ the plane in London but he flew on to Manchester. *(land)*

e They ______________________ to the concert but their parents paid for it so they could. *(not go)*

f The film ______________________ better than the book but it wasn't. *(be)*

g I ______________________ Jane when I was in London. She will be angry with me because I didn't. *(visit)*

h Tom ______________________ curry for his guests but he gave them fish and chips instead. *(make)*

i You ______________________ to school; it was quicker than the bus today. *(walk)*

j Sheila ______________________ me yesterday but she had to go to the doctor's. *(phone)*

k He ______________________ to school yesterday; he had a very bad cold. *(not go)*

l Without Mike's help, we ______________________ our work. *(not finish)*

m It's too late now but I think we ______________________ a bigger car. *(buy)*

Topic 14: The Glastonbury Festival

A

In the mid 1960s music festivals started to be organised for young people. Woodstock, which was held in America in 1969, is perhaps the most famous one of all time. Older people didn't like the festivals since they were noisy and young "hippies" drank too much and took drugs.

B

Since Woodstock, one of England's largest music festivals has been happening regularly on a farm in the south of England. Michael Eavis was an ordinary farmer who enjoyed music like most young people. One day he watched a Blues festival not far from his village of Pilton and this gave him the idea of using his land for a music festival, too. In 1970, he organised his first one which was small and had a few problems but generally was enjoyed by everyone. In the following year a second free festival was held; its name was the Glastonbury Fair. This time the groups were better known and about 12,000 people arrived. However, this was the last festival at Worthy Farm until 1979.

C

The Glastonbury Festival, though, really began in 1981 when it attracted 30,000 people. The people who lived in Pilton didn't like the festival at first – like Woodstock, they complained of noise, traffic, alcohol and drugs – but they soon saw that it was well-organised and brought a lot of money to businesses in the area, so they accepted it. The new festival had changed from the earlier ones; different styles of music were played, art events were held and many other things, too, from clothes stalls to exhibitions about 'green' living.

D

Every year the number of people coming to Glastonbury has increased and the names of the bands playing have become bigger and bigger; today, the superstars of the world of music regularly appear. Glastonbury Festival is now one of the biggest musical events in Britain, over 100,000 people come to the weekend event and tickets are often sold out within hours of being on sale.

E

Farmers give their land a rest every few years. If the land is used every year, it becomes tired and eventually not very good. Eavis knows this, of course, so every five years there isn't a festival. This helps the land to stay good for future festivals and it gives the people in the village a rest from them, too.

Questions on the text

113 Answer the following questions about the text.
Write full sentences where possible.

a Why were some people unhappy about the first music festivals?

____

b Write the name of the farmer, the name of the farm and the village where the Glastonbury Festival takes place.

farmer: ____________________ farm: ____________________

village: ____________________

c "The first festival was free." Is this sentence true or false? Say why.

☐ true
☐ false

Why: ____

____

d When wasn't there a Glastonbury Festival for a long time?

____

e Tick (✓) the correct answer.

The village people …

☐ have complained about every festival since they started.
☐ soon saw that the festival had advantages for them.
☐ try to stop the festival every five years.

f Name three things that happen at Glastonbury Festival.

____

g What type of artists now comes to the festival?

____

h Why is it difficult to get a ticket for the festival?

____

i Why isn't there a festival now every year?

____

114 Give each paragraph a heading from the list. There are two headings which you don't need. Write the letter of each paragraph (A–E) next to the best heading.

Heading	Paragraph
The farmer and his festival	
Badly organised	
Hugely successful	
A quiet year	
The weather	
Festival origins	
Everyone is happy	

Grammar

Was sind Relativsätze?

Relativsätze sind Nebensätze, die sich auf ein bestimmtes Nomen aus dem Hauptsatz beziehen und dieses näher erläutern.

Beispiel: The girl who wrote the letter lives in New York.

Wie kannst du einen Relativsatz ersetzen?

Du kannst einen Relativsatz mit *who*, *which* oder *that* durch ein Partizip ersetzen. Es gibt zwei Möglichkeiten:

- Du ersetzt den Relativsatz durch das ***present participle*** (-*ing*-Form). Die -*ing*-Form hat **aktive Bedeutung**.
  Beispiel: The plane which goes to London is late. *(relative clause)*
  → The plane going to London is late. *(present participle)*
- Du ersetzt den Relativsatz durch das ***past participle***. Das *past participle* hat **passive Bedeutung**.
  Beispiel: The camera which is left on the table is Mike's. *(relative clause)*
  → The camera left on the table is Mike's. *(past participle)*

Wie kannst du Partizipien im Satz noch verwenden?

Partizipien können wie Adjektive Nomen näher bestimmen. Sie stehen vor dem Nomen, auf das sie sich beziehen.

Beispiele: The ringing phone was annoying. *(present participle)*
Karen's lost watch was soon found. *(past participle)*

115 Use a participle construction to replace the relative clauses in the following sentences.

a The people who went to Woodstock were hippies.

____

b Many people who complained about the festival were old.

____

c The man who organised the first Glastonbury Festival was a farmer.

____

d The free festivals which were held at Worthy Farm were the first two.

____

e The people who live in Pilton like the festival.

____

f The bands that play today are usually very famous ones.

____

g The ticket which was found at the entrance was mine.

____

h The people who help at Glastonbury are volunteers.

____

i The money which is taken at the festival is usually used for a good project.

____

j The number of visitors that come to Glastonbury has increased.

____

k The people who work at the festival are often students.

____

l The exhibitions which give information about green products are very popular.

____

m The land which is used at Worthy Farm needs a rest every five years.

____

116 Complete the gaps in the comic with a participle or a relative clause.
Use the following words, but in English. The words are also not in the correct order.
benutzen – bringen – halten – eine Panne haben – schlafen – spielen

Vocabulary

117 Read the explanation of each word and look at the German meaning, too. Try to complete the English words, which all have something to do with pop festivals, with their missing vowels (a – e – i – o – u).

English word	explanation	German word
__ __ d __ __ nc __	the people who go to watch a pop festival, a film or a theatre show	*Publikum / Zuschauer*
b __ sy	full – lots of people	*(hier) voll*
cr __ wd	a lot of people	*(Menschen-)Menge / Zuschauermenge*
p __ rf __ rm __ r	the person who sings or dances, for example	*Künstler(in) / Musiker(in)*
r __ bb __ sh	what is often left on the ground when everyone goes home – it should go into bins	*Müll*
s __ c __ r __ ty	the people or the situation which makes everyone safe at a big concert, for example	*Sicherheit*
st __ ge	where the band play or actors act	*Bühne*
t __ ck __ t	what you need to get into a concert, a film or a play, for example	*Eintrittskarte*

118 Build one sentence about a pop concert with each new word.

a The ______________________ loved the band.

b ____

c ____

d ____

e ____

f ____

g ____

h ____

Using your English

119 Would you like a large pop festival where you live?

a What are the advantages and disadvantages of that? Make a mind map.

b Write about 120 words about this topic.

Test

120 Write the following sentences using a participle construction or a participle as an adjective.

a

The band that played first was not very good.

b

A bus which went to the concert broke down.

c

The rubbish which is left after the concert has to be collected.

d

The performers who arrived this morning are well known.

e

Judy's tent which collapsed was old.

f

The camera which was lost at the festival was Ian's.

g

The large crowd who visited the concert left quietly last night.

h

The glasses which broke were Charlie's.

Topic 15: Pier 39

Fisherman's Wharf is one of San Francisco's many attractions where, near the end of the 19th century, fishermen from Italy began arriving and started new businesses there. Although some fishermen still do go out in their boats from the Wharf, the main business here is now tourism.

Although Fisherman's Wharf has super restaurants and views across San Francisco Bay towards the prison island of Alcatraz, it is the sea lions on Pier 39 which attract most visitors and entertain them. The sea lions' story fascinates many people.

Before the San Francisco Loma Prieta earthquake in 1989 there were no sea lions at Fisherman's Wharf at all, then suddenly a few started to arrive. In the following year about 50 sea lions climbed onto the pontoons in the harbour, their numbers then exploded to 300 in just a few months. The sea lion population continued to increase and by 2009, 1,700 were counted. But as quickly as they came, they left again.

Scientists think that the reason the sea lions arrived in such large numbers and then went again was because of the fish. When the fish swam away the sea lions had to, too.

The sea lions have now returned to Pier 39 again and tourists from all over the world spend many hours watching them play on the pontoons and barking at each other. The sea lions are protected; you are not allowed to feed them or annoy them in any way. They can be aggressive if you get near them and they are big: up to two metres and weighing almost 400 kilos.

Although sea lions can be a problem most people would rather have them at Pier 39 for ever; and there's a good chance of that. They like routine so even if they leave for a short time they will probably return. Unfortunately, though, rubbish in the sea is a big danger for them. Hopefully somebody will do something about this soon.

Vocabulary

wharf (line 1): *Kai*
pier (line 7): *Pier/Landungsbrücke*
pontoon (line 11): *Steg*
(to) bark (line 22): *(hier) brüllen*

Questions on the text

121 Which statements are *true, false* or *not in the text*? Tick (✓) the box and explain your true and false answers.

	true	false	not in the text
a The Italians brought tourism with them.	☐	☐	☐
b There are not many fishermen left at the Wharf.	☐	☐	☐
c If you want to visit Alcatraz, you can from Fisherman's Wharf.	☐	☐	☐
d The sea lions came after an earthquake.	☐	☐	☐
e At first there were about 300 sea lions.	☐	☐	☐
f Something probably suddenly frightened the sea lions away.	☐	☐	☐
g There are a lot of pontoons at Fisherman's Wharf.	☐	☐	☐

h The sea lions are fun to watch. ☐ ☐ ☐

____

____

i A cleaner sea would help the sea lions. ☐ ☐ ☐

____

____

Grammar

Wann verwendest du den Infinitiv ohne to?

Du verwendest den Infinitiv ohne *to*:

- nach *had better* (‚sollte').
  Beispiele: You had better drive slowly.
  People had better not put rubbish in the sea.
- nach *would rather* (‚möchte lieber').
  Beispiele: I would rather sit over there.
  I would rather not play tennis today.
- mit dem Ausdruck *(to) let somebody do something*. Der Ausdruck bedeutet ‚jemanden etwas tun lassen', ‚jemandem erlauben, etwas zu tun', ‚zulassen, dass jemand etwas tut'.
  Beispiele: We let Michael take our photos.
  We didn't let Jane walk home alone.
- mit dem Ausdruck *(to) make somebody do something*. Dieser Ausdruck bedeutet ‚jemanden veranlassen, etwas zu tun', ‚jemanden zwingen, etwas zu tun', ‚jemanden dazu bringen, etwas zu tun'.
  Beispiele: Theresa made David carry her heavy bag.
  Simon didn't make Carol help him.

122 Complete the gaps in the story. Use the grammar that you have just looked at.

Pam ________________ Jerry take her to Pier 39; he didn't really want to go. She wanted to throw the sea lions something to eat. Jerry said, "First, you ________________ ask someone if you can feed the sea lions."

Pam asked someone and, of course, the person at Pier 39 ________________ Pam feed them. That wasn't allowed, but he ________________ her take lots of photos.

It was a very hot day and Jerry didn't like the sun. He told Pam that he ________________ sit in the shade *(Schatten)* while she watched the sea lions. Jerry sat there for 30 minutes but then decided he ________________ go shopping. Pam ________________ Jerry leave most of his money with her because she didn't want him to spend a lot.

> Du verwendest den Infinitiv ohne *to* auch:
> - nach (modalen) Hilfsverben.
>   *Beispiele:* We shall fly to America.
>   We could stay in a nice hotel.
>   We didn't go in August.
> - nach *would* als Ausdruck einer Gewohnheit in der Vergangenheit. Du kannst *would* mit einem Handlungsverb anstelle von *used to* verwenden.
>   *Beispiel:* He would go for a walk every night before he went to bed.
> - nach *do*, wenn du das Verb betonen willst.
>   *Beispiel:* I don't like horror films, but I do like comedies.
> - nach einem Verb der Sinneswahrnehmung (z. B. *see, hear, watch*) + Objekt, wenn du ausdrücken möchtest, dass die Handlung abgeschlossen ist bzw. dass die Handlung von Anfang bis Ende wahrgenommen wird/wurde.
>   *Beispiel:* She watched him walk into the bank.
>
>   Wenn du hingegen ausdrücken möchtest, dass die Handlung noch nicht abgeschlossen ist und du deren Verlauf betonen möchtest, so verwendest du statt des Infinitivs die *-ing*-Form.
>   *Beispiel:* She watched him swimming in the river.

123 Look at the German words in brackets before completing the sentences in English.

a They ________________ direct to America. *(fliegen können)*

b An hour ago, I ________________ Georgina ________________ the door. *(hören/öffnen)*

c They don't like walking in the mountains, but they ________________ walking on the beach. *(genießen – betont)*

d Tony ________________ the car ________________ quickly. *(sehen/anhalten)*

e My father was funny. He ______________________ a hat every day even when it was hot. *(gewöhnlich tragen)*

f I ______________________ that you ______________________ Harry today. *(glauben – betont/sollte anrufen)*

g We ________________ Gill ________________ this morning. *(hören/singen)*

h ________________ you ________________ Aunty Wendy in America, too? *(besuchen können)*

Vocabulary

124 How good are you with opposites? Look at some parts of the text from page 134 and write the opposite of the word in **bold print** The opposite must be able to be used in the sentence.

a … one of San Francisco's **many** attractions …

____

b … near the **end** of the 19th century …

____

c … Fisherman's Wharf has **super** restaurants …

____

d … **fascinates** many people.

____

e … there were **no** sea lions at Fisherman's Wharf …

____

f … then **suddenly** a few started to arrive …

____

g … arrived in such **large** numbers …

____

h … sea lions have now **returned to** Pier 39 …

____

i They **like** routine …

____

Using your English

125 Creative writing: Look at the photo carefully and read through the text and the grammar again. Imagine that you took the picture. Continue the story in about 120 words – try to include at least one part of the grammar.

When we were in San Francisco, we went to Pier 39.

Test

126 Complete the dialogue using the words in the two lists.
The lists are not in the correct order.

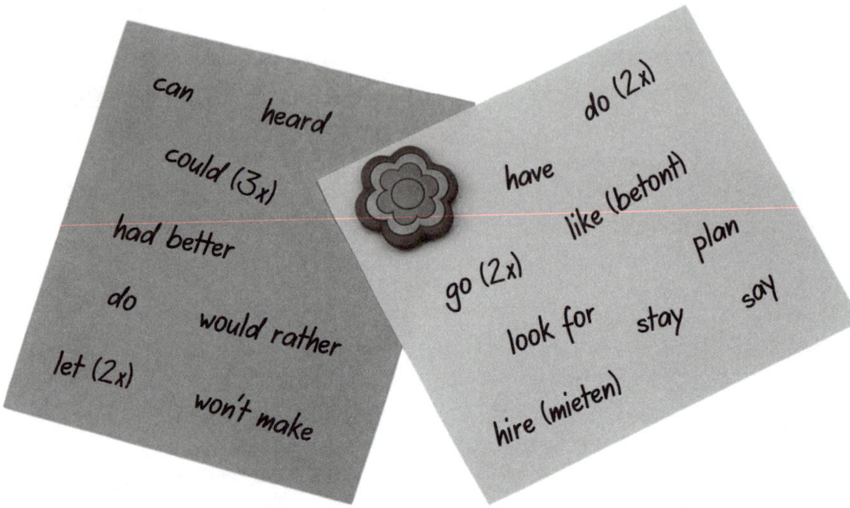

Mum: I think that we should ______________ Robbie ______________ our holiday this year.

Janice: He ____________________________ it well. I don't want a horrible one.

Robbie: We ____________________________ to California again. I enjoyed that last year.

Dad: I think Robbie's idea is super. We ________________________ a camper van.

Robbie: No, thanks. I ____________________________ in hotels.

Janice: Me, too.

Dad: Okay. I __________________ you _________________ a holiday in one – it's just that I _________________ them. But, you ____________________ some nice hotels, Robbie.

Robbie: Okay, but where?

Mum: I _________________ someone __________________ New England was nice. We ____________________ there.

Janice: That's a great idea. _______________ us _______________ that.

Vocabulary

Auf den folgenden Seiten findest du eine alphabetisch geordnete Liste der Wörter und der unregelmäßigen Verben, die in diesem Buch vorkommen. Die Vokabelliste enthält sowohl britische als auch amerikanische Schreibung und einige schwierige grammatikalische Ausdrücke.
Vokabeln lernst du am besten regelmäßig und in Sechser- oder Siebenergruppen. Mache zwischen deinen Lerneinheiten konsequent kleine Pausen, damit sich die neuen Vokabeln „setzen" können.

- Du kannst die dir unbekannten Wörter in der Vokabelliste und im Text markieren. Dann fallen sie dir sofort auf, wenn du das Buch aufschlägst und du wiederholst sie ganz automatisch.
- Du kannst die Vokabelliste auch dazu verwenden, deinen gesamten Wortschatz zu wiederholen. Decke eine Spalte mit einem Blatt Papier ab und schreibe die entsprechenden deutschen oder englischen Wörter oder die unregelmäßigen *simple-past-* und *past-participle*-Formen auf ein Blatt. Überprüfe danach genau, ob du die englischen Wörter richtig geschrieben hast.
- Du kannst schwierigere Vokabeln auch auf Karteikärtchen schreiben: dann kannst du sie überall hin mitnehmen und wiederholen, wenn du Zeit hast.

Wortschatz 9. Klasse Realschule

* = *irregular verb*	
adj.	Adjektiv
adv.	Adverb
AE	amerikanisches Englisch
BE	britisches Englisch
pl.	Plural
sg.	Singular

a, an	ein(e)
about	über, ungefähr, etwa
above	über
(to) accept	akzeptieren, annehmen
accident	Unfall
across	über
(to) act	(Theater) spielen, sich benehmen, handeln
active sentence	Aktivsatz
activity	Aktivität
actor	Schauspieler
(to) add	addieren, hinzufügen
address	Adresse
adjective	Adjektiv
(to) admit	zugeben
advantage	Vorteil
adverb	Adverb
advert	Werbung, Anzeige
advice	Rat
(to) advise	raten, einen Rat geben
a few	einige, ein paar
(to) afford	sich leisten
(to be*) afraid of	Angst haben vor, sich fürchten vor
Africa	Afrika
after	nach
afternoon	Nachmittag
again	noch einmal, wieder
aggressive	aggressiv, angriffslustig
ago	vor
(to) agree	zustimmen
ahead	vorn
aim	Ziel
air	Luft
alcohol	Alkohol
alive	lebendig
all	alle, ganz
all kinds	jede Art
all over	überall
(to) allow	erlauben
almost	beinahe, fast
alone	allein
along	entlang
a lot	viel
a lot of	viel(e), eine Menge
already	bereits, schon
also	auch, außerdem
alternative	Alternative
although	obwohl
always	immer
a.m.	vormittags
America	Amerika
American	Amerikaner(in), amerikanisch
amount	Menge
and	und
and so on	und so weiter
angry	verärgert, wütend
angst	Angst
animal	Tier
(to) annoy	belästigen, ärgern, stören

annoyed	verärgert
annoying	lästig, nervig, störend
another	noch ein(e/r/s), ein(e) andere(r/s)
answer	Antwort
(to) answer	antworten
answer phone	Anrufbeantworter
any	(irgend)welche, jede(r/s)
anyone, anybody	(irgend)jemand, jeder
anything	(irgend)etwas
anywhere	irgendwo
(to) apologise	sich entschuldigen
(to) appear	erscheinen, scheinen
appointment	Termin
area	Gegend, Gebiet
argument	Streit, Auseinander-setzung
Arizona	Arizona *(Staat in den USA)*
arm	Arm
around	um … herum
(to) arrive	ankommen
art	Kunst
article	Artikel
artist	Künstler
art work	Kunstwerk
as	als
as soon as	so schnell wie
as well	auch
(to) ask	fragen
at	an, auf, in, bei
at all	überhaupt
at first	zuerst, anfangs
at least	wenigstens
at night	am Abend
at the moment	im Moment, im Augenblick
(to) attempt	versuchen
(to) attract	anziehen
attraction	Attraktion
attractive	attraktiv

audience	Zuschauer, Publikum
August	August
aunt	Tante
Aunty (Rita)	Tante (Rita)
autograph	Autogramm
available	erhältlich, verfügbar
average	Durchschnitt
(to) avoid	meiden
(to be*) aware	sich bewusst sein
awareness	Bewusstsein
away	weg, fort
awful	schrecklich

back	Rücken, zurück
back pocket	Gesäßtasche
backwards	rückwärts
bacon	Speck
bad, badly *(adv.)*	schlecht
badminton	Federball, Badminton
bag	Tasche
(to) bake	backen
ball	Ball, Kugel
band	Band, Popgruppe
bank	Bank *(Geldinstitut)*
barbecue	Grillfest
(to) bark	*(hier)* brüllen
basic (word)	Grund(wort)
bath	Bad
battery	Batterie
battle	Schlacht
(to) be*	sein
(to) be* able to	können
(to) be* careful	vorsichtig sein
beach	Strand
beautiful	(wunder)schön, wundervoll
(scenic) beauty	landschaftliche Schönheit
beauty centre	Kosmetiksalon
because	weil
(to) become*	werden
beefburger	Beefburger

before	bevor, vor, vorher
(to) begin*	anfangen, beginnen
beginning	Anfang, Beginn
behind	hinter
(to) believe	glauben
bell	Glocke, Klingel
(to) belong to	gehören zu
below	unten, unter
best	beste(r/s)
better	besser
between	zwischen
bicycling	Fahrradfahren
big	groß
bike	Fahrrad
bin	Mülleimer
Biology	Biologie
birthday	Geburtstag
birthday card	Geburtstagskarte
birthday wishes	Geburtstags-glückwünsche
black	schwarz
blackboard	Tafel
blue	blau
Blues	Blues
boat	Boot, Schiff
(to) boil	kochen
bold print	Fettdruck
book	Buch
(to) book	buchen
border	Grenze
(to) bore	langweilen
both	beide
bottle	Flasche
bottom	Boden, Talsohle
box	Kästchen, Kasten
boy	Junge
brackets	Klammern
bread	Brot
(to) break*	(zer)brechen, kaputtgehen
(to) break* down	eine Panne haben
(to) break* into	einbrechen in
breakfast	Frühstück
brick	Ziegelstein
bridge	Brücke
(to) bring*	bringen, mitbringen
British	Brite, Britin, britisch
brochure	Broschüre
brother	Bruder
brown	braun
buggy	Buggy, Kinder(sport)-wagen
(to) build*	bauen
builder	Bauarbeiter(in), Bauherr(in)
building	Gebäude
bus	Bus
bus stop	Bushaltestelle
bus trip	Busreise
business	Geschäft
businessman	Geschäftsmann
busy	beschäftigt
but	aber
butterfly	Schmetterling
button	Knopf
(to) buy*	kaufen
by	von, neben
(to go*) by boat	mit dem Schiff (fahren)
(to go*) by bus	mit dem Bus (fahren)
(to do*/make*) by hand	von Hand (machen)
(to go*) by lorry	mit dem Lastwagen (fahren)
café	Café
cake	Kuchen
California	Kalifornien
call	Ruf, Anruf
(to be*) called	heißen
camera	Kamera
campaign	Kampagne
camper van	Wohnmobil
can	können

(to) cancel	absagen
cannot	nicht können
can't stand	nicht leiden können
canyon	Canyon, Schlucht
captain	Kapitän
car	Auto
car park *(BE)*	Parkplatz
carbohydrates	Kohlenhydrate
(to take*) care	aufpassen
careful	vorsichtig, sorgfältig
carefully *(adv.)*	aufmerksam, sorgfältig, vorsichtig
carpet	Teppich
carrot	Möhre, Karotte
(to) carry	tragen
castle	Burg
(to) catch*	fangen
(to) catch* (a bus)	(einen Bus) erreichen
(to) cause	verursachen
(to) celebrate	feiern
cell phone *(AE)*	Handy
Celsius	Celsius
centimetre	Zentimeter
centre	Zentrum
century	Jahrhundert
ceramics	Keramik
chair	Stuhl
chance	Chance, Gelegenheit, Möglichkeit
change	Veränderung
(to) change	(ver)ändern, tauschen, auswechseln
chapter	Kapitel
(to) chat	chatten
cheap	billig
cheddar cheese	Cheddar Käse
cheese	Käse
chicken	Huhn
child (*pl.* children)	Kind
Chinatown	Chinatown *(Chinesisches Viertel in einer Stadt)*
Chinese	chinesisch, Chinese, Chinesin
chips	Pommes frites
chocolate	Schokolade
choice	Wahl
(to) choose*	(aus)wählen
Christmas	Weihnachten
cinema	Kino
circle	Kreis
(to) circle	umkreisen, einkreisen
city	Großstadt
class	Klasse
classroom	Klassenzimmer
clay	Ton
(to) clean	putzen
(to be*) clean	sauber (sein)
clear, clearly *(adv.)*	klar, deutlich
clever	klug
(to) climb	klettern
climbing wall	Kletterwand
(to) close	schließen
clothes *(pl.)*	Kleidung
cloud	Wolke
coast	Küste
coat	Jacke
coffee	Kaffee
coin	Münze
cold	kalt
(to be*) cold	kalt sein
(to) collapse	zusammenbrechen
(to) collect	sammeln, abholen
colour	Farbe
colourful	bunt
(to) come*	kommen
(to) come* from	stammen
(to) come* out of	herauskommen aus
comic	Comic, Bildgeschichte
comment	Kommentar, Stellungnahme, Bemerkung
(to) communicate	mitteilen, in Verbindung stehen
community	Gemeinde

company	Unternehmen
(to) compare	vergleichen
competition	Wettbewerb
(to) complain (of)	sich beschweren, sich beklagen, klagen (über)
(to) complete	vervollständigen, ergänzen
complete, completely *(adv.)*	vollständig, völlig
computer	Computer
concert	Konzert
concrete	Beton
condition	Zustand
(to) connect	verbinden
(to) consider	in Betracht ziehen
construction	Konstruktion
(to) contact	kontaktieren, sich wenden an
(to) continue	weitermachen
(to) cook	kochen
cool	kühl
corner	Ecke, *(hier)* Biegung
(to) correct	korrigieren, verbessern
correct, correctly *(adv.)*	richtig
(to) cost*	kosten
cougar	Puma, Berglöwe
could	könnte(n), könntest, konnte
(to) count	zählen
country	Land
countryside	Landschaft, Natur
course	Kurs
(to) cover	bedecken, Schutz suchen
(to) crawl	krabbeln
credit card	Kreditkarte
(to) cross	überqueren
crossing	Kreuzung
crowd	Menge
culture	Kultur
(to) curl	(hier) zusammenrollen
curry	Curry
curtain	Vorhang
curve	Kurve
(to) cut*	schneiden
(to) cycle	Fahrrad fahren
Dad, dad	Vater
dam	Staudamm
(to) damage	beschädigen
(to) dance	tanzen
danger	Gefahr
dangerous	gefährlich
(the) dark	(die) Dunkelheit
dark	dunkel
date	Datum, Jahreszahl
daughter	Tochter
day	Tag
(to) deal* with	handeln, befassen, Geschäfte machen mit
(to) decide	entscheiden
(to) decorate	tapezieren, streichen
deep	tief
deer	Reh, Hirsch
(to) defrost	auftauen
delegate	Delegierte(r)
(to) describe	beschreiben
desert	Wüste
design	Design, Entwurf
(to) design	entwerfen, entwickeln
designer	Designer(in)
(to) desire	wünschen
desk	Schreibtisch
(to) destroy	zerstören
(to) develop	entwickeln
device	Gerät
diagram	*(hier)* Zeichnung
dialogue	Dialog
(to) die	sterben
difference	Unterschied

different, differently *(adv.)*	unterschiedlich, anders
difficult	schwierig
(to) dig*	graben
(to) dig* out of	ausgraben aus
dinner	Essen, Mittagessen, Abendessen
direction	Richtung
direct speech	direkte Rede
dirty	schmutzig, dreckig
disadvantage	Nachteil
(to) disagree	nicht einig sein, widersprechen
(to) disallow	nicht erlauben, nicht zulassen
(to) disconnect	abschalten
(to) dislike	nicht mögen
(to) display	aushängen, ausliegen
divided by	geteilt durch
(to) do*	tun, machen
doctor	Arzt, Ärztin
dog	Hund
door	Tür
dot	Punkt
down	abwärts, herunter
downhill	bergab
drama	Drama, Schauspiel, Schauspielerei
dramatic	dramatisch
(to) draw*	zeichnen
(to) dream*	träumen
(to) drink*	trinken
(to) drive*	fahren
(to) drop	fallen lassen
drug	Droge
during	während
each	jede(r/s)
each other	einander, gegenseitig
early	früh
earthquake	Erdbeben
earthquake awareness poster	*(etwa) Poster, das über das richtige Verhalten bei einem Erdbeben informiert*
east	Osten
easy, easily *(adv.)*	leicht
(to) eat*	essen
e-diary	Tagebuch auf dem Computer
egg	Ei
eight	acht
either	entweder
electrician	Elektriker(in)
electricity	Strom
electrolyte drink	mineralhaltiges Getränk, Elektrolytgetränk
e-mail	E-Mail
(to) e-mail	eine E-Mail schreiben/senden
emergency	Notfall
empty	leer
(to) encourage	ermutigen
end	Ende
ending (of a sentence)	Satzende
engine	Motor
engineer	Ingenieur(in)
England	England
English	englisch
(to) enjoy	genießen
enjoyable	angenehm
enough	genug
(to) enter	eintreten
(to) entertain	unterhalten
entrance	Eingang
(diary) entry	(Tagebuch-)Eintrag
e-pal	*(etwa) Freund(in), mit dem/der man im E-Mail-Austausch steht*
equipment	Ausrüstung
equivalent	Entsprechung

especially	besonders
even	auch, sogar
evening	Abend
event	Veranstaltung
eventually	schließlich, endlich
ever	jemals
every	jede(r/s)
everybody, everyone	jeder, alle
everything	alles
everywhere	überall
exactly	genau
example	Beispiel
exciting	aufregend
excuse me	Entschuldigung, Verzeihung
exercise	Übung
exhibition	Ausstellung
(to) expect	erwarten
expensive	teuer
expert	Experte, Expertin
(to) explain	erklären
explanation	Erklärung
(to) explode	explodieren, schnell ansteigen
(to) explore	erforschen, erkunden
expression	Ausdruck
extra	zusätzlich
extremely	äußerst, überaus, außerordentlich
eye	Auge
face	Gesicht
fact	Tatsache
factory	Fabrik
(to) fail	scheitern, versagen
(summer) fair	(Sommer-)Fest
(to) fall*	fallen, stürzen
(to) fall* down	hinfallen, stürzen
(to) fall* off	herunterfallen
(to) fall* over	umfallen, hinfallen
false	falsch

family	Familie
famous	berühmt
(to) fancy doing something	Lust haben, etwas zu tun
fantastic	fantastisch, wundervoll
far *(adj./adv.)*	weit
farm	Bauernhof
farmer	Bauer, Bäuerin
(to) fascinate	faszinieren
fast *(adj./adv.)*	schnell
father	Vater
February	Februar
(to) feed*	füttern
(to) feel* good	sich gut fühlen
festival	Festival, Fest
few	wenige
(a) few	einige
field	Feld
fifty	fünfzig
(to) fight*	kämpfen
(to) fill in	ausfüllen
film	Film
film star	Filmstar
finally	endlich
(to) find*	finden
(to) find* out	herausfinden
finger	Finger
(to) finish	beenden
fire	Feuer
fireman	Feuerwehrmann
firm	Firma
first	erste(r/s)
first aid	Erste Hilfe
fish	Fisch
fisherman	Fischer, Angler
fishing	Fischfang
(to) fit	passen, einbauen
fitness studio	Fitness-Studio
five	fünf
flat	Wohnung, flach
flight	Flug

flight attendant	Flugbegleiter(in)
floor	Stockwerk, Boden
flower	Blume
(to) fly*	fliegen
flying	Fliegen
(to) follow	folgen
following	folgende(r/s)
food	Essen
foot (*pl.* feet)	Fuß
football	Fußball
football team	Fußballmannschaft
for	für, seit
for example	zum Beispiel
(to) force	zwingen
forest	Wald
(to) forget*	vergessen
fork	Gabel
form	Form, Art
four	vier
four-star hotel	Vier-Sterne-Hotel
fourth	vierte(r/s)
fragile area	gefährdetes Gebiet
France	Frankreich
free	kostenlos
free time	Freizeit
freeway *(AE)*	Autobahn
(to) freeze*	(ge)frieren
French	französisch, Franzose, Französin
frequent, frequently *(adv.)*	häufig
fresh	frisch
friend	Freund(in)
friendly *(adj.)*	freundlich
(to) frighten … away	*(hier)* verscheuchen
from	von
front door	Haustür
frozen	gefroren, tiefgefroren
(to) fry	braten
full	voll
fun	Spaß
funny	lustig, komisch
furniture	Möbel
further	weiter
future	Zukunft
galleon	Galeone *(Schiff)*
gallery	Galerie
gap	Lücke
garage	Garage, Werkstatt
garbage *(AE)*	Müll
garden	Garten
garden hut	Gartenhütte
gate	Tor
generally	normalerweise, im Allgemeinen
general store *(AE)*	Gemischtwarenladen
geometrical	geometrisch
German	Deutsche(r), deutsch
(the) Germans	die Deutschen
Germany	Deutschland
(to) get*	bekommen, gelangen
(to) get* off (a bus)	(aus einem Bus) aussteigen
(to) get* out (of a car)	herauskommen, (aus einem Auto) aussteigen
(to) give*	geben
(to) give* up	aufgeben, verzichten auf
glass	Glas
glasses *(pl.)*	Brille
Glastonbury	*(Stadt in England)*
(to) go*	gehen
(to) go* on	weitermachen, weitergehen
goat	Ziege
(to be*) going to	werden
go-karting	Gokart Fahren
golf	Golf
good	gut
(to be*) good at	in … gut sein

Grand Canyon	*(Schlucht im Südwesten der USA, durch die der Colorado River fließt)*
grandad	Großvater, Opa
grandma	Großmutter, Oma
grandparents	Großeltern
grass	Gras
(to) grate	reiben
great	großartig, toll
(to) grill	grillen
ground	Boden
group	Gruppe
guest	Gast
guide book	Reiseführer
hair	Haar(e)
hairdresser	Friseur(in)
half	halb, Hälfte
half an hour	eine halbe Stunde
(sport) hall	(Sport-)Halle
ham	Schinken
hand	Hand
handball	Handball
(a) handful (of)	(eine) Handvoll ...
handy	praktisch, nützlich
(to) happen	geschehen
happy	glücklich
harbour	Hafen
hard	hart
Harvard University	*(Universität in den USA)*
hat	Hut, Mütze
(to) hate	hassen
(to) have*	haben
(to) have* a barbecue	grillen
(to) have* got	haben, besitzen
(to) have* to	müssen
he	er
head	Kopf

headline	Schlagzeile, Überschrift
(to) hear*	hören
heat	Hitze
heavy	schwer
helicopter	Hubschrauber
help	Hilfe
(to) help	helfen
her	ihr(e), sie
here	hier
Hermits Rest	*(Ort im Grand Canyon National Park)*
herself	sich, selbst
hi	hallo
(to) hide*	verstecken
high	hoch
high winds	starker/kräftiger Wind
highway *(AE)*	Bundesstraße
(to) hike	wandern
hill	Hügel
him	ihn, ihm
himself	sich, selbst
Hindi	Hindi *(Sprache)*
hippy	Hippie
(to) hire	mieten
his	sein(e)
historic	historisch
history	Geschichte
(to) hold*	halten, abhalten
(to) hold* on	festhalten
(to) hold* together	zusammenhalten
hole	Loch
holiday	Ferien, Urlaub
Hollywood Bowl	*(Amphitheater bei Los Angeles)*
home	Zuhause
(to) hope	hoffen
hopefully *(adv.)*	hoffentlich
horrible	scheußlich, schrecklich

horse	Pferd
horse riding	Reiten
hot	heiß
hot dog stand	Hotdogstand
hotel	Hotel
hour	Stunde
house	Haus
how	wie
How about ...?	Wie wäre es mit ...?
however	jedoch, aber
how long	wie lang
how many	wie viele
how much	wie viel
huge	riesig
hugely *(adv.)*	ungeheuer, sehr
hundred	hundert
hungry	hungrig
(to) hurt	schmerzen, wehtun, verletzen
hut	Hütte
I	ich
ice cream	Eis
idea	Idee
if	wenn, falls, ob
ill	krank
illegal	illegal
illogical	unlogisch
illustration	Illustration
(to) imagine	sich vorstellen
immature	unreif, kindisch
immediately	sofort
imperfect	fehlerhaft
important	wichtig
impossible	unmöglich
(to be*) impressed	beeindruckt sein
(to) improve	verbessern
in	in
in front of	vor
in order to	um ... zu
in spite of	trotz
inclement	*(hier)* rau
(to) include	*(hier)* einarbeiten
(to) increase	zunehmen, anwachsen
India	Indien
indoor	Innen-
infinitive	Infinitiv
information *(sg.)*	Information(en)
infrequently *(adv.)*	selten
ingredient	Zutat
inhabitant	Einwohner, Bewohner
(to) injure	verletzen
injury	Verletzung
insect	Insekt
(to) insert	*(hier)* einwerfen
(on the) inside	(im) Inneren
inside	innen, drinnen
(software) installation	(Software-)Installation
instead	stattdessen
instead of	statt, anstelle von
instruction	Anweisung
(to) intend	beabsichtigen, vorhaben
interest	Interesse
(to be*) interested in	an ... interessiert (sein)
interesting	interessant
(the) interior	(das) Innere
internet	Internet
internet site	Website
into	in, hinein
(to) introduce	einführen
introduction	Einführung
introductory	einleitend
(to) invent	erfinden
invention	Erfindung
(to) invite	einladen
island	Insel
issue	Problem, Angelegenheit
it	es
Italian	Italiener(in), italienisch

italics	Kursivschrift
Italy	Italien
its	sein(e), ihr(e)
itself	sich, selbst
jacket potato	Ofenkartoffel
jeans *(pl.)*	Jeans
jewellery	Schmuck
job	Arbeit, Tätigkeit, Beruf
(to) jog	joggen
journey	Reise
July	Juli
(to) jump into	hineinspringen, einsteigen in
June	Juni
just	gerade, nur
(to) keep*	halten, behalten
Kenya	Kenia
key	*(hier)* Lösung
kiln	Brennofen
kilo	Kilo
kilometre	Kilometer
kind	Sorte, Art
kind regards	viele Grüße, mit freundlichen Grüßen
knife (*pl.* knives)	Messer
(to) know*	wissen, kennen
(to be*) known	bekannt (sein)
L.A.	Los Angeles
(to) label	beschriften
lake	See
Lake District	*(Seen- und Berglandschaft im Nordwesten Englands)*
land	(Bau-)Land
(to) land	landen
landscape	Landschaft
language	Sprache
laptop	Laptop

large	groß
last	der/die/das letzte
late	spät
(to be*) late	sich verspäten
later	später
(to) laugh	lachen
layout	Layout
(to) lead*	anführen
leaf (*pl.* leaves)	Blatt
(to) learn*	lernen
(to) leave*	verlassen, abfahren, weggehen
(to) leave* a message	eine Nachricht hinterlassen
left	links, übrig
leg	Bein
legal	legal
leisure	Freizeit
(to) lend*	(ver)leihen
letter	Brief, Buchstabe
library	Bibliothek
(to) lie*	liegen
(to) lie* down	sich hinlegen
life	Leben
lifestyle	Lebensstil
lift	Lift, Fahrstuhl
light	Licht, leicht
(to) like	mögen, gern haben
like	wie
line	Linie, *(AE)* Warteschlange
list	Liste
(to) listen	zuhören
litre	Liter
little	wenig, klein
(to) live	leben, wohnen
living room	Wohnzimmer
logical	logisch
logo	Logo
long	lang
(to) look	schauen, sehen, ansehen

(to) look after	sich kümmern um, aufpassen auf
(to) look at	ansehen
(to) look for	nach ... suchen/schauen
(to) look forward to	sich freuen auf
(to) look good	gut aussehen
(to) look like	wie ... aussehen
(to) look out of	aus ... schauen
loop	Schleife
lorry	Lastwagen
(to) lose*	verlieren
lots of	viel, viele
loud	laut
(to) love	lieben, sehr mögen
Love from ...	Liebe Grüße von ...
lovely *(adj.)*	schön, herrlich
low	niedrig
lucky	glücklich
lunchtime	Mittagsstunde

machine	Maschine
made out of	aus ...
magazine	Zeitschrift
main	Haupt-
(to) make*	machen
man	Mann
(to) manage	schaffen
many	viele
map	Karte
(to) marry	heiraten
(to) match	zusammenpassen, zuordnen
materials	Materialien
mature	reif
may	können, dürfen
maybe	vielleicht, möglicherweise
mayonnaise	Mayonnaise
me	mir, mich
meal	Mahlzeit
(to) mean*	bedeuten
meaning	Bedeutung
mechanic	Mechaniker(in)
(to) meet*	treffen
meeting	Treffen, Besprechung
(to) mention	erwähnen
mesa	*(Tafelberg)*
message	Nachricht
metal	Metall
metre *(BE)*	Meter
metre-high	meterhoch
Mexico	Mexiko
microwave	Mikrowelle
(to) microwave	etwas in der Mikrowelle erwärmen
mid	Mitte
midday	Mittag
(in the) middle of	in der Mitte von
might	könnte
mile	Meile
million	Million
(don't) mind	(nichts gegen) etwas einzuwenden haben
mind map	Mind-Map
Mind the tenses.	Achte auf die Zeiten.
mine	meine(r/s)
minute	Minute
mirror	Spiegel
mischief	Unfug
(to) miss	vermissen, verpassen, vermeiden
missing	fehlend
mistake	Fehler
(to) mix	mischen
mobile (phone) *(BE)*	Handy
modern art	moderne Kunst
Mojave Desert	*(Wüste im Südwesten der USA)*
Monday	Montag
money	Geld
month	Monat

more	mehr
morning	Morgen
most	am/die meisten
mother	Mutter
motorway *(BE)*	Autobahn
mountain bike	Mountainbike
mountain lion	Puma, Berglöwe
(to) move	(sich) bewegen, umziehen
(to) move into	einziehen in
much	viel
Mum, mum	Mutter, Mama
museum	Museum
music	Musik
musical	Musical
must	müssen
mustn't	nicht dürfen
my	mein(e)
nail	Nagel
name	Name
(to) name	nennen
narrowest	schmalste(r/s)
national park	Nationalpark
Native American	Indianer(in)
native speaker	Muttersprachler
Navajo Council	*(Regierung der Navajo-Indianer)*
near	in der Nähe von, nahe
necessary	notwendig
neck	Hals
(to) need	brauchen
need to	etwas tun müssen
needn't	nicht müssen, nicht brauchen
negative	verneint
neighbour	Nachbar
neither	auch nicht
(to) network	etwas vernetzen
never	niemals
never mind	macht nichts
new	neu
New Mexico	New Mexico *(Staat in den USA)*
news	Nachricht(en)
newspaper	Zeitung
next	(als) nächste(r/s)
next to	neben
nice	nett, schön
night	Nacht
nightly *(adj./adv.)*	jede Nacht
nine	neun
no	nein, kein
no one	niemand, keiner
noise	Lärm
noisy	laut
non-stop	Nonstop-, durchgehend
nor	auch nicht
normal	normal
normally *(adv.)*	normal, normalerweise
not	nicht
nothing	nichts
now	jetzt
number	Nummer, Zahl
nurse	Krankenschwester, Krankenpfleger
object	Ding, Objekt
occasionally *(adv.)*	gelegentlich
... o'clock	... Uhr
October	Oktober
of	von
of course	natürlich, selbstverständlich
(to) offer	anbieten
official language	Amtssprache
often	oft
OK, okay	okay
old	alt
on	auf
on sale	zu verkaufen
on top of	(oben) auf

once	einmal
one	ein
one, ones	einzige(r/s), einzig
online	Online
only	nur, bloß
onto	auf
(to) open	öffnen
open day	Tag der offenen Tür
opinion	Meinung
opposite	gegenüber, Gegenteil
or	oder
orange	*(hier)* Orange *(Farbe)*
order	Reihenfolge
(to) order	befehlen, bestellen
ordinary	gewöhnlich, normal
(to) organise	organisieren
organiser	Organisator(in)
origin	Ursprung, Herkunft
original	Original
Oscars	*(Filmpreis)*
other	andere(r/s)
otherwise	anderenfalls
ought to	sollte
our	unser(e)
ourselves	uns, selbst
outside	draußen, außen
(the) outside	(die) Außenseite
over	über
over there	dort drüben
(of one's) own	eigene(r/s)
owner	Besitzer

packet	Paket, Schachtel
page	Seite
paint	Farbe
(to) paint	malen, streichen
painter	Maler
(piece of) paper	(Blatt) Papier
paper clip	Büroklammer
paragraph	Absatz, Abschnitt
parents	Eltern
park	Park
(to) park	parken
parking lot *(AE)*	Parkplatz
parking meter	Parkuhr
part	Teil
part of	(ein) Teil von
participle	Partizip
partly *(adv.)*	teilweise, zum Teil
party	Party, Feier
passive	Passiv
past	Vergangenheit
path	Weg, Pfad
pattern	Muster
pavement *(BE)*	Gehsteig, Bürgersteig
(to) pay*	zahlen
pay station *(AE)*	Parkautomat
PC	PC
peace	Frieden
pedestrian	Fußgänger(in)
pen	Stift
peninsula	Halbinsel
people	Leute, Menschen
per	pro
perfect	perfekt
performance	Aufführung, Vorstellung
performer	Künstler(in)
perhaps	vielleicht
period	Zeitspanne
periodically	regelmäßig
(to) permit	erlauben
person	Person
(to) persuade	überreden, überzeugen
pet	Haustier
(to) phone	anrufen
phone	Telefon
phone number	Telefonnummer
photo(graph)	Foto(grafie)
photographer	Fotograf(in)
phrase	Ausdruck
piano	Klavier
(to) pick up	abholen, in die Hand nehmen

picnic	Picknick
picture	Bild
piece of cake	Stück Kuchen
pier	Pier, Landungsbrücke
pilot	Pilot(in)
pin	(Ansteck-)Nadel
pineapple	Ananas
(to) pitch it *(AE)*	wegwerfen
pizza	Pizza
place	Ort
(to) place	*(hier)* stellen
plan	Plan
(to) plan	planen
plane	Flugzeug
plant	Pflanze
(to) play	spielen
please	bitte
plenty of	eine Menge, viel, viele
plinth	Plinthe, Sockel
p.m.	nachmittags
pocket	Tasche
police	Polizei
policeman	Polizist
pontoon	Steg, Ponton
pop festival	Popfestival
pop group	Popgruppe
popular	beliebt
population	Bevölkerung
positive	bejaht, positiv
possibility	Möglichkeit
possible	möglich
possibly *(adv.)*	möglicherweise
(to) post	schicken
poster	Poster
post office	Postamt
pot	Topf
potato	Kartoffel
power	Strom
practical	praktisch
(to) practise	üben
prawn	Garnele
(to) prefer	lieber mögen
prefix	Präfix, Vorsilbe
(to) prepare	vorbereiten
present	Geschenk
presentation	Präsentation, Vortrag
(to) press	drücken
pretty	hübsch
price	Preis
prison	Gefängnis
private	privat
probably	wahrscheinlich
problem	Problem
product	Produkt
profile	Profil
programme	Programm
project	Projekt
(to) promise	versprechen
pronoun	Pronomen
(to) protect	beschützen
protection	Schutz
protector	Beschützer
Pueblo Acoma	*(Stadt in New Mexico, USA)*
puma	Puma
pupil	Schüler
(to) push	schieben
pushchair *(BE)*	Kinderwagen
(to) put*	setzen, stellen, legen
(to) put* into	hineinsetzen, -legen, -stellen
quarter of an hour	Viertelstunde
question	Frage
question word	Fragewort
queue *(BE)*	Warteschlange
(to) queue	Schlange stehen
(to be*) quick	schnell (sein)
quickly *(adv.)*	schnell
quiet, quietly *(adv.)*	ruhig
quite	ziemlich

race	Rennen
railroad *(AE)*	Eisenbahn
railway *(BE)*	Eisenbahn
rain	Regen
ramp	Rampe
ranger	Ranger
rather	eher, lieber, vielmehr
rather ... than	lieber ... als
(to) reach	erreichen
(to) read*	lesen
ready	fertig, bereit
ready-made	gebrauchsfertig
really	wirklich
reason	Grund
receipt	Quittung, Empfangsbestätigung
receptionist	Mitarbeiter(in) am Empfang
recipe	(Koch-)Rezept
(to) recommend	empfehlen
red	rot
(to) refer to	sich beziehen auf
regularly	regelmäßig
relative clause	Relativsatz
(to) remember	sich erinnern
(to) remind	erinnern
repair	Reparatur
(to) repair	reparieren
(to) replace	ersetzen, zurückstellen
reply	Antwort
(to) reply	antworten
report	Bericht
(to) report	berichten
reported speech	indirekte Rede
reporter	Reporter(in)
rescue	Rettung
(to) rescue	retten
rescuer	Retter(in)
(to) reserve	reservieren
responsible	verantwortlich
(the) rest	(der) Rest
rest	Pause, Erholung

(to) rest	(sich) erholen
restaurant	Restaurant
(to) return	zurückkommen, zurückgeben
rich	reich
(fair) ride	(Karussell-)Fahrt
(to) ride*	reiten, fahren
(turn) right	rechts (abbiegen)
right *(adj./adv.)*	richtig, rechts
rim	Rand
(to) ring	klingeln, anrufen
(to) risk	riskieren, wagen
river	Fluss
road	Straße
(to) roast	rösten, (Fleisch) braten
rock	Fels
rock music	Rockmusik
Rocky Mountains	*(Bergkette in Nordamerika)*
roller coaster	Achterbahn
room	Zimmer, Platz
round	rund
route	Strecke, Route
Route 66	*(berühmte Straße in den USA)*
routine	Routine
rubbish *(BE)*	Abfall, Müll
rule	Regel
(to) run*	laufen
(to be*) sad	traurig (sein)
safe	sicher
safety	Sicherheit
(to) sail	segeln, (Boot) fahren
sailing	Segeln
sale	Verkauf, Ausverkauf
sales assistant	Verkäufer(in)
salty	salzig
same	derselbe, dieselbe, dasselbe
sandwich	belegtes Brot, Sandwich

Saturday	Samstag
sausage	Wurst
(to) save	sparen, retten
(to) say*	sagen
(to) scan	einscannen
(to) scare	erschrecken, Angst machen
(to be*) scary	furchterregend (sein)
scenic	landschaftlich (schön)
schadenfreude	Schadenfreude
school	Schule
scientist	Wissenschaftler(in)
scissors *(pl.)*	Schere
sculpture	Skulptur
sea	Meer
sea level	Meeresspiegel
sea lion	Seelöwe
second	Sekunde, zweite(r/s)
section	Teil
security	Sicherheit
(to) see*	sehen
(to) seem	scheinen
seldom	selten
(to) sell*	verkaufen
(to) send*	schicken, senden
sensible	vernünftig
sentence	Satz
September	September
service	Service, Kundendienst
(to) set*	setzen, stellen
(to) set* off	losfahren, aufbrechen
(to) set* out	aufbrechen
shade	Schatten
shape	Form
she	sie
shelter	Schutz
(to) shelter	Schutz suchen, schützen
(to) shine*	scheinen
(to) shock	schockieren
shoe	Schuh
shop	Geschäft
(to) shop	einkaufen
shop assistant	Verkäufer(in)
(to go*) shopping	einkaufen (gehen)
short	kurz
should	sollte
show	Show
(to) show	zeigen
side	Seite
sidewalk *(AE)*	Bürgersteig, Gehsteig
sights	Sehenswürdigkeiten
sign	Schild, Zeichen
similar	ähnlich
simple	einfach
since	seit
(to) sing*	singen
singer	Sänger(in)
single	einzeln
siren	Sirene *(≈ verführerische Dame)*
sister	Schwester
(to) sit*	sitzen
situation	Situation
six	sechs
sixty	sechzig
size	Größe
skateboard	Skateboard
skin	Haut
Sky City	*(Stadt in New Mexico, USA)*
(to) sleep*	schlafen
slice of (bread)	Scheibe (Brot)
slow, slowly *(adv.)*	langsam
small	klein
(to be*) smart	schlau (sein)
(to) smoke	rauchen
snake	Schlange
(to) snow	schneien
so	also, so
sofa	Sofa
soft	weich
software	Software
(to be*) sold out	ausverkauft (sein)

soldier	Soldat(in)
(to) solve	lösen
some	etwas, einige, ein paar
someone	(irgend)jemand
something	(irgend)etwas
sometimes	manchmal
somewhere	irgendwo
soon	bald
(to be*) sorry	bedauern, sich entschuldigen
(to) sound	läuten, klingen
sound system	Stereoanlage, Hi-Fi-Anlage
south	Süden
south of	südlich von
South Africa	Südafrika
souvenir	Andenken, Souvenir
space	Raum, Platz
space number	*(hier)* Parkplatznummer
spaghetti bolognese	Spaghetti Bolognese
(to) speak*	sprechen, reden
special	besondere(r/s)
specific	bestimmt
(to) spell*	buchstabieren
spelling	Rechtschreibung
(to) spend*	(Zeit) verbringen, (Geld) ausgeben
sport	Sport
sports centre	Sportzentrum
(to) spray	sprühen
square	Quadrat
squash	Squash
stairs *(pl.)*	Treppe
stage	Bühne
stall	Stand, Bude
stand	Stand
(to) stand*	stehen
star	Stern
start	Start
(to) start	starten, anfangen
state	Staat
statement	Aussage
station	Bahnhof
Statue of Liberty	Freiheitsstatue
(to) stay	übernachten, bleiben
(to) steal*	stehlen
step	Stufe, Schritt
still	noch, immer noch
stomach ache	Bauchschmerzen
stone	Stein
stone block	Steinblock
(to) stop	anhalten, stehenbleiben, nicht stattfinden lassen
(to) stop to do sth./doing sth.	aufhören, etwas zu tun
store	Geschäft
storm	Sturm
story	Geschichte
straight	gerade
strange	seltsam
street	Straße
street map	Stadtplan
string	Schnur
stroller *(AE)*	Kinder(sport)wagen
strong	stark
student	Student, Schüler
(to) study	studieren
style	Stil
subject	Subjekt
subway *(AE)*	Unterführung, U-Bahn
successful, successfully *(adv.)*	erfolgreich
such as	so wie, zum Beispiel
suddenly	plötzlich
(to) suffer	leiden
(to) suggest	vorschlagen
suitable	passend, geeignet
summer	Sommer
sun	Sonne
Sunday	Sonntag

sunny	sonnig	temperature	Temperatur
sunshine	Sonnenschein	temporary	*(hier)* Aushilfs-, Aushilfe
super	super, toll	ten	zehn
supermarket	Supermarkt	tennis	Tennis
superstar	Superstar	tense	Zeitform
(to be*) sure	sicher (sein)	tent	Zelt
(to) surf	surfen	terrible	schrecklich, furchtbar
surfing	Surfen	(to) test	prüfen
(to be*) surprised	überrascht (sein)	text	Text
survival	Überleben	(to) text	eine SMS schreiben
(to) survive	überleben	text message	SMS
survivor	Überlebende(r)	than	als *(im Vergleich)*
sweets	Süßigkeiten	(to) thank	danken, sich bedanken
(to) swim*	schwimmen	thank you	danke
swimming pool	Schwimmbad	thanks	danke
synonym	Synonym	that	dass, jene(r/s), der, die, das (dort), *(Relativpron.)* der, die, das
(computer) system	(Computer-)System	the	der, die, das
table	Tisch	theatre	Theater
tactic	Taktik	their	ihr(e)
(to) take*	nehmen	them	sie, ihnen
(to) take* a photo	ein Foto machen	themselves	sich, selbst
(to) take* care	aufpassen	then	damals
(to) take* from	mitnehmen	there	dort, da
(to) take* something off	etwas ausziehen	therefore	deshalb, deswegen
(to) take* place	stattfinden	there is, there are	es gibt
a talk	Besprechung	these	diese
(to) talk	reden, sprechen	they	sie
(to) talk about	über ... sprechen	thin	dünn
(to) talk to	sprechen mit	thing	Sache, Gegenstand, Ding
task	Aufgabe	(to) think*	denken
(to) taste	schmecken	(to) think* about	nachdenken über
Tate Modern	*(Kunstmuseum in London)*	thirty	dreißig
(to) teach*	unterrichten	this	diese(r/s)
teacher	Lehrer(in)	those	jene
technology	Technologie, Technik	though	obwohl, dennoch
telephone	Telefon	three	drei
television	Fernsehen		
(to) tell*	sagen, erzählen		

through	über, durch
(to) throw*	werfen
thunderstorm	Gewitter
(to) tick	abhaken
ticket	Ticket, Karte
tidy	ordentlich
(to) tidy up	aufräumen
(to) tie	schließen, fesseln, (ver)binden
thief	Dieb(in)
time	Zeit
time of day	Tageszeit
tin	Zinn, Dose
tip	Spitze, Tipp
(to be*) tired	müde sein
(to be*) tired of	(etwas/jemanden) satt haben
title	Titel
to	in, nach
toast	Toast
toast Hawaii	Toast Hawaii
today	heute
together	zusammen
tomorrow	morgen
tonight	heute Abend, heute Nacht
too	auch, zu
top	Spitze, oben
top (designers)	Top (Modedesigner)
topic	Thema
totally	vollkommen
tour	Tour, Rundfahrt, Rundgang, Besichtigung
tourism	Tourismus
tourist	Tourist(in)
towards	in Richtung, nach, zu
town	Stadt
track	Rennbahn, Fahrweg
traditional	traditionell
Trafalgar	*(Seeschlacht, die 1805 stattfand)*
Trafalgar Square	*(Platz in London)*
traffic	Verkehr
train	Zug
(to) translate	übersetzen
translation	Übersetzung
(to) travel	reisen
treasure	Schatz
tree	Baum
triangle	Dreieck
tribal	Stammes-
tribe	Stamm
trip	Reise, Fahrt
true	wahr
(to) try	versuchen
(to) try out	ausprobieren
T-shirt	T-Shirt
Tuesday	Dienstag
tuna	Thunfisch
(to) tune (a car)	(ein Auto) tunen
(to) turn	abbiegen
(to) turn around	sich umdrehen
(to) turn something	etwas umdrehen
TV	Fernseher
(to watch) TV	fernsehen
twelve	zwölf
twenty	zwanzig
twenty-four	vierundzwanzig
twenty-one	einundzwanzig
twice	zweimal
two	zwei
type	Art
typical	typisch

umbrella	Regenschirm
unclear	unklar
under	unter
(the) Underground *(BE)*	*U-Bahn in London*
(to) underline	unterstreichen
(to) understand*	verstehen
undiscovered	unentdeckt

unemployed	arbeitslos
unfortunately	unglücklicherweise
unhappy	unglücklich
uniform	Uniform
uninterrupted	ununterbrochen
United Kingdom	Vereinigtes Königreich
unless	außer wenn
unsafe	nicht sicher, gefährlich
untidy	unordentlich
until	bis
unusual	ungewöhnlich
uphill	bergauf
up to now	bis jetzt
us	uns
(the) use	Verwendung, Benutzung
(to) use	benutzen, gebrauchen
(to be* no) use	nichts bringen, nichts nutzen
(to be*) used to	gewohnt (sein)
useful	nützlich
usually	gewöhnlich
van	(Klein-)Bus
variation	Variante, Abweichung
vegetable	Gemüse
vehicle	Fahrzeug
Venice Beach	*(Strand in Los Angeles)*
verb	Verb
very	sehr
vet	Tierarzt, Tierärztin
vet's assistant	Tierarzthelfer(in)
view	Ausblick
village	Dorf
virus	Virus
visit	Besuch
(to) visit	besuchen, besichtigen
visitor	Besucher(in)
vocabulary	Wortschatz, Vokabeln, Vokabelverzeichnis
volunteer	Freiwillige(r)
vowel	Vokal
(to) wait	warten
waiter	Kellner
Wales	Wales
walk	Spaziergang, Spazierweg
(to) walk	laufen, gehen
Walk of Fame	Walk of Fame *(Gehweg in Los Angeles)*
wall	Mauer
(to) want	wollen
warm	warm
(to) warn	warnen
warning	Warnung
(to) wash	waschen
watch	Armbanduhr
(to) watch	sehen, beobachten
water	Wasser
wavy	wellig
way	Weg
we	wir
(to) wear*	tragen
weather	Wetter
weather forecast	Wettervorhersage
website	Website
wedding	Hochzeit
Wednesday	Mittwoch
week	Woche
weekend	Wochenende
(to) weigh	wiegen
well *(adv.)*	gut
well-known *(adj.)*	bekannt
west	Westen
western	West- , westlich
wet	nass
wharf	Kai
what	was
What about ...?	Wie wäre es mit ...?
wheel	Rad
when	wann, wenn, als
whenever	jedes Mal,wenn
where	wo
whether	ob

which	welche(r/s)
while	während
white	weiß
who	wer
whole	ganz
whose	wessen
why	warum
wide	weit
wife	Ehefrau
wild	wild
wildlife	Tierwelt
will	werden
(to) win*	gewinnen
window	Fenster
windsurfing	Windsurfen
wish	Wunsch
with	mit, bei
within	innerhalb
without	ohne
woman	Frau
(to) wonder	sich fragen
wood	Holz
Woodstock	*(Musikfestival)*
word	Wort
work	Arbeit
(to) work	arbeiten
(not) work	nicht funktionieren
work of art	Kunstwerk
world	Welt
(to) worry	sich Sorgen machen
worst	schlechteste(r/s), schlimmste(r/s)
(to be*) worth	wert (sein)
would	würde
would like	möchte gern
would love/ like to do	möchte gern etwas tun
(to) wrap up	einpacken
(to) write*	schreiben
wrong	falsch

year	Jahr
... years old	... Jahre alt
yellow	gelb
yes	ja
yesterday	gestern
yet	bis jetzt
(not) yet	noch nicht
you	du, dich, dir, ihr, euch, Sie, Ihnen, man
your	dein, euer, Ihr
yours	deine(r/s), eure(r/s), Ihre(r/s)
yourself	dich, sich, selbst
young	jung

Irregular verbs

infinitive	simple past	past participle	deutsche Übersetzung
(to) be	was/were	been	*sein*
(to) become	became	become	*werden*
(to) begin	began	begun	*anfangen, beginnen*
(to) break	broke	broken	*(zer)brechen, kaputtgehen*
(to) bring	brought	brought	*bringen, mitbringen*
(to) build	built	built	*bauen*
(to) buy	bought	bought	*kaufen*
(to) catch	caught	caught	*fangen*
(to) choose	chose	chosen	*(aus)wählen*
(to) come	came	come	*kommen*
(to) cost	cost	cost	*kosten*
(to) cut	cut	cut	*schneiden*
(to) deal with	dealt with	dealt with	*handeln, befassen, sich beschäftigen mit*
(to) dig	dug	dug	*graben*
(to) do	did	done	*tun, machen*
(to) draw	drew	drawn	*zeichnen*
(to) dream	dreamt/dreamed	dreamt/dreamed	*träumen*
(to) drink	drank	drunk	*trinken*
(to) drive	drove	driven	*fahren*
(to) eat	ate	eaten	*essen*
(to) fall	fell	fallen	*fallen, stürzen*
(to) feed	fed	fed	*füttern*
(to) feel	felt	felt	*fühlen*
(to) fight	fought	fought	*kämpfen*
(to) find	found	found	*finden*
(to) fly	flew	flown	*fliegen*
(to) forget	forgot	forgotten	*vergessen*
(to) freeze	froze	frozen	*(ge)frieren*
(to) get	got	got	*bekommen, gelangen*
(to) give	gave	given	*geben*

(to) go	went	gone	*gehen*
(to) have	had	had	*haben*
(to) hear	heard	heard	*hören*
(to) hide	hid	hidden	*verstecken*
(to) hold	held	held	*halten, abhalten*
(to) hurt	hurt	hurt	*schmerzen, wehtun, verletzen*
(to) keep	kept	kept	*halten, behalten*
(to) know	knew	known	*wissen, kennen*
(to) lead	led	led	*anführen*
(to) learn	learnt/learned	learnt/learned	*lernen*
(to) leave	left	left	*verlassen, abfahren, weggehen*
(to) lend	lent	lent	*(ver)leihen*
(to) lie	lay	lain	*liegen*
(to) lose	lost	lost	*verlieren*
(to) make	made	made	*machen*
(to) mean	meant	meant	*bedeuten*
(to) meet	met	met	*treffen*
(to) pay	paid	paid	*zahlen*
(to) put	put	put	*setzen, stellen, legen*
(to) read	read	read	*lesen*
(to) ride	rode	ridden	*reiten, fahren*
(to) run	ran	run	*laufen*
(to) say	said	said	*sagen*
(to) see	saw	seen	*sehen*
(to) sell	sold	sold	*verkaufen*
(to) send	sent	sent	*schicken, senden*
(to) set	set	set	*setzen, stellen*
(to) shine	shone	shone	*scheinen*
(to) sing	sang	sung	*singen*
(to) sit	sat	sat	*sitzen*
(to) sleep	slept	slept	*schlafen*

infinitive	simple past	past participle	deutsche Übersetzung
(to) speak	spoke	spoken	*sprechen, reden*
(to) spell	spelt/spelled	spelt/spelled	*buchstabieren*
(to) spend	spent	spent	*(Zeit) verbringen, (Geld) ausgeben*
(to) stand	stood	stood	*stehen*
(to) steal	stole	stolen	*stehlen*
(to) swim	swam	swum	*schwimmen*
(to) take	took	taken	*nehmen*
(to) teach	taught	taught	*unterrichten*
(to) tell	told	told	*sagen, erzählen*
(to) think	thought	thought	*denken*
(to) throw	threw	thrown	*werfen*
(to) understand	understood	understood	*verstehen*
(to) wear	wore	worn	*tragen*
(to) win	won	won	*gewinnen*
(to) write	wrote	written	*schreiben*

Key

- Im *Key* findest du die **Lösungen zu allen Aufgaben**. Hier solltest du erst nachsehen, wenn du eine Aufgabe bzw. ein *Topic* vollständig bearbeitet hast.
- Damit du dich schneller zurechtfindest, sind viele der Lösungen **fett hervorgehoben**.
- In einigen Aufgaben sind mehrere Lösungen richtig. Die verschiedenen Lösungsmöglichkeiten sind durch Schrägstriche voneinander getrennt. In Klammern stehende Wörter oder Satzteile kannst du auch weglassen.
- Die Lösungen zu den Schreib-Aufgaben können dir wertvolle Ideen für deine Textproduktion liefern. Denk aber daran, dass sie als Vorschlag zu verstehen sind. Lass dich deshalb nicht verunsichern, wenn deine Lösung von der hier angegebenen abweicht!
- Prüfe bitte auch deine Rechtschreibung genau! Wenn deine Lösung falsch war, solltest du die Übung später noch einmal wiederholen.

Topic 1: Sky City

1 **a** Only one Native American tribe is different.

This sentence is [ ] true
[✓] false

because in the text it says (**that**) **each tribe is different**.

b Pueblo Acoma / Sky City

c Where is the village?

A [✓]

B [ ]

C [ ]

d Which photograph shows the village?

A [ ]

B [✓]

C [ ]

e A man cannot have a house in this village.

This sentence is [✓] true
[ ] false

because in the text it says (**that**) **the houses in the village belong to the women**.

f Which pattern is not one from this village?

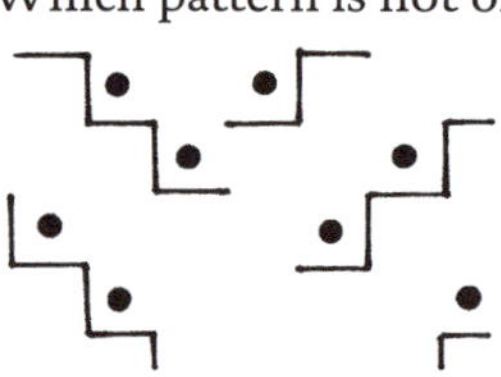

A [ ]

B [ ]

C [✓]

g The typical colours used are red, black, white and blue.

This sentence is ☐ true
☑ false

because in the text it says **(that) the colours are usually only black, white, brown, red and orange**.

h The clay which is used …

- ☐ is bought in the next town.
- ☐ comes from the mesa.
- ☑ comes from a different area.
- ☐ takes a long time to be cleaned.

i Where do some colours come from?

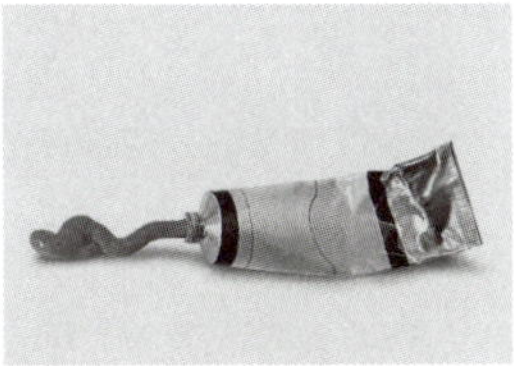

A ☐

B ☑

C ☐

j
- ☐ Each pot takes sixty hours to make.
- ☑ Some pots take sixty hours to make.
- ☑ After the pot is painted it is put into a kiln.
- ☐ Before the pot is painted it is put into a kiln.

2
- a We sometimes **watch** a film at home in the evenings.
- b Today we **are going** to Pueblo Acoma.
- c If you **visit** New Mexico, you must buy something from the Native Americans.
- d It **is** very hot in New Mexico and Arizona.
- e I **am writing** an e-mail now to my brother.
- f **Do** you **like** the pot that I bought?
- g It **is** so warm today.
- h Jo **is taking** a photo of Sky City at the moment.
- i The museum **closes** at 6 p.m.

3

a Four people **are sitting** on their horses.
b At the moment they **aren't riding** them.
c One horse **doesn't have / hasn't got** anyone on it.
d One man **is standing** next to a horse.
e I **like / am enjoying** the view.
f The people **are looking** at the view.
g Usually people **take** a lot of photos when they **are** here.
h The sun **is shining** today.
i I **think** the sun must shine here every day.

4

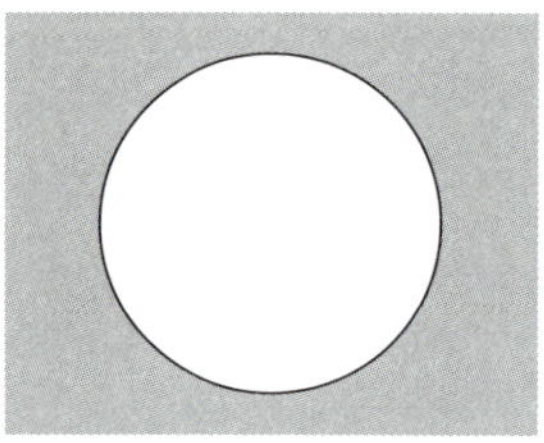

circle

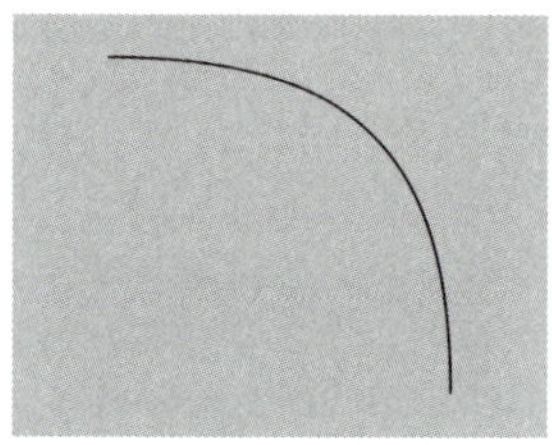

curve

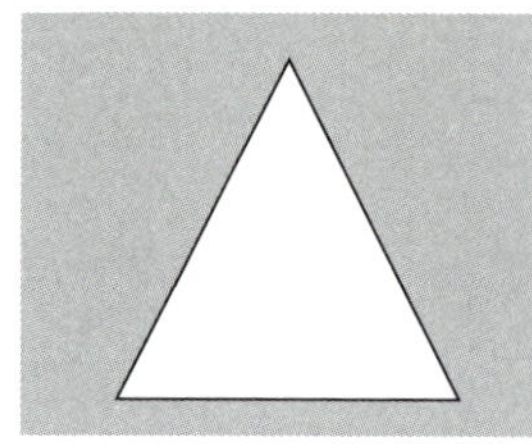

triangle

square

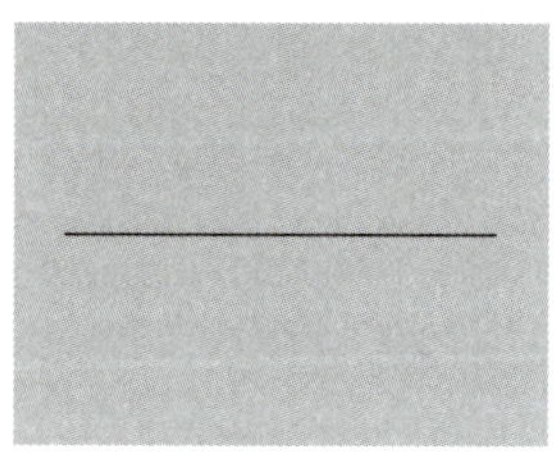

straight line

butterfly shape

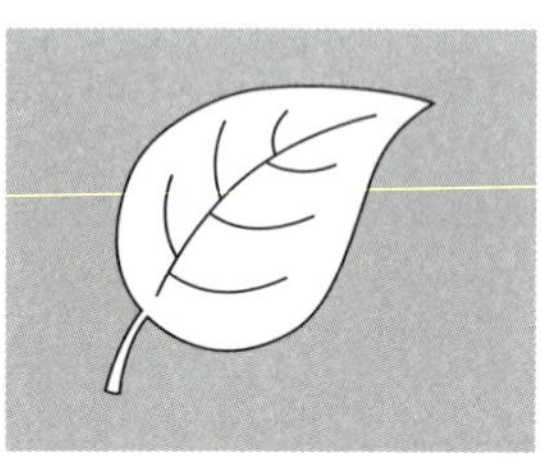

leaf shape

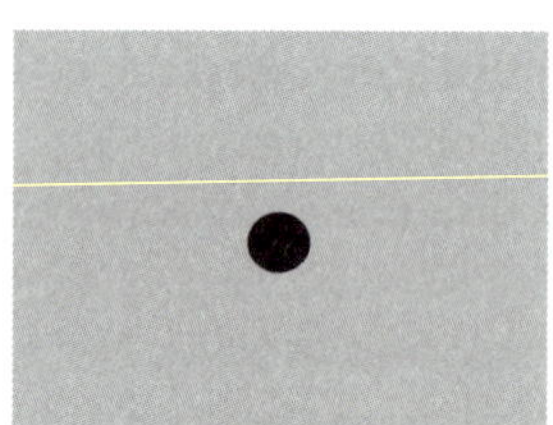

dot

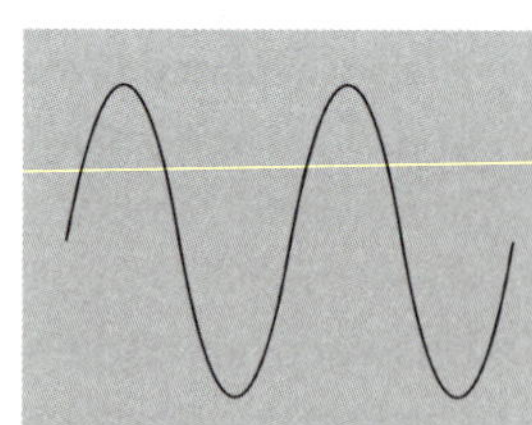

wavy line

5 *(example answer)*
Hi Sally. I've just bought a great pot in Sun City. It's round and on one side there is a design with a lot of straight lines on it. On the other side there are different shapes; some look like leaves or maybe a butterfly. You can see some steps. These are clouds and the dots on the pot are the rain.

6 **a** George **comes** from New Mexico. He **is** a Native American and his family **live(s)** in Pueblo Acoma. At the moment George **is helping** his sister, Andrea. She **is painting** a beautiful pattern on a pot but she can't finish it – she **needs** more paint.

b When George **visits** his family, Andrea often **asks** him to find the plants and rocks she **uses** for the paint.

c George's best friend in Acoma is Mike. Mike **doesn't make** pots, he makes jewellery.
"Hi, Mike. What **are you doing**?" says George.
"I'**m reading** an interesting book about traditional jewellery," answers Mike.
"I **like** that type of jewellery, too," says George.
"You don't normally **stay** this long, George," says Mike.
"That **is** true," answers George. "But, I **am meeting** Martina in Flagstaff on Wednesday and then we **are travelling** home together. The train **leaves** in the afternoon."

Topic 2: Where's London Bridge?

7 **a** long and thin
b a rich businessman
c water sports
d he bought/buy the peninsula and the (desert) land around it
e in 1963
f they quickly brought lots of people to the city/to bring people to the city/ to attract people to the city
g it was in a (very) bad condition
h by boat and by lorry
i in 1971
j for small planes (to start and land)

8

a Show where the dam is and what happened to the river.

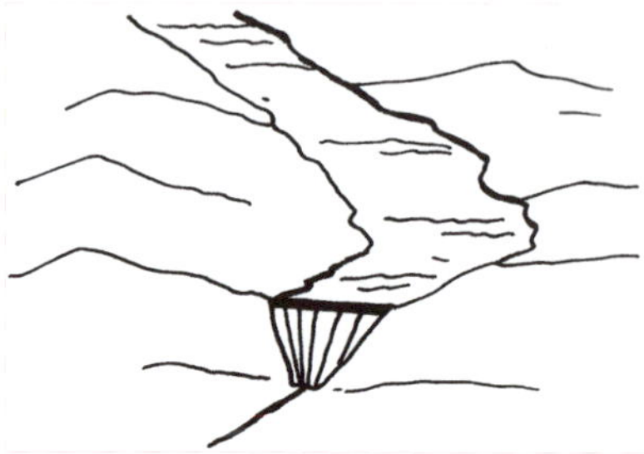

b Show the area that McCulloch bought.

c Show exactly where the bridge came from.

d Show how the bridge got to America.

e Show where the bridge went and what happened.

f Show another McCulloch idea.

9 Hi Aunty Kathy,
Sorry – we **were swimming** when you phoned – never mind.
We **arrived** yesterday after a long journey. While Mum **was driving**, Dad **was sleeping** – typical! I **stayed** in my room last night but Matthew **went** for a walk. He **was taking/took** photos of the bridge until 11 p.m.! He **showed** me the photos before breakfast.
While we **were eating** breakfast, I **remembered** that it was your birthday. Happy birthday from us.
Love from everyone.

10
- a We haven't eaten yet.
- b Mum hasn't been swimming this morning.
- c I've just been talking to Aunt Kathy for half an hour.
- d I haven't spoken to her since Christmas.
- e How long have you been waiting?
- f I've been sitting here for ten minutes.
- g Dad has loved boats since our holiday on one in France.
- h He has wanted a boat for years.

11

Hi Sara,
After I **had phoned** you, I **went** to the swimming pool, too. Thanks for the birthday wishes. How are you all? K.

Hi Aunty Kathy,
It **had been** too hot to walk very far the day before but it **was** cooler this morning. So, after we **had walked** across London Bridge we **went** to the lake. But by lunchtime we **had seen** everything and it **was** very hot again. We **had already decided** to leave today so we just **left** a few hours earlier. S.

12
- a We **have been** in America for ten days now.
- b My father **had driven** a long way before we **came** to a bridge across the Colorado River.
- c The river soon **became** a long, thin lake.
- d I **saw** boats on the lake and some people **were swimming** in it.
- e People **have lived/have been living** in Lake Havasu City since 1963.
- f While we **were walking** to the bridge it **was** still 40 ° Celsius.
- g I **returned** to our hotel and **went** to the swimming pool.

13 *(example answers)*

a subject: a shop
verbs: sell, **buy, enter**
adverbs or adjectives: colourful, **funny, small, friendly**

b subject: **beach**
verbs: **swim, sit, walk**
adverbs or adjectives: **hot, long, busy**

c subject: **group / band**
verbs: **play, sit, sing**
adverbs or adjectives: **good, warm, loud**

d subject: **hot dog stand**
verbs: **taste, buy, queue**
adverbs or adjectives: **good, large, popular**

14 *(example answer)*

There were a lot of small shops near the beach. One of them was selling lots of colourful and funny T-shirts, so we entered it and had a look around. The people in the shop were very friendly and we bought some T-shirts there. Near the shop, there was a band playing in the street. They played very good music and the singer had a brilliant voice. He even sang one of my favourite songs! It was very warm and they were sitting under an umbrella. We listened to them playing for a while and then decided to go to the beach. Their music was so loud that we could still hear it from far away!
Venice Beach is a very long beach. As the weather was great, it was very busy. A lot of young people were swimming in the sea. It was a hot, sunny day and I saw a lot of people walking there, too. Opposite the beach there was a popular hot dog stand. Their hot dogs were large and tasted very good. A lot of people were queuing for them.

15

a Yesterday we …

- [x] bought
- [ ] have bought
- [ ] had bought

… some hats.

b After we …

- [ ] walk
- [ ] were walking
- [x] had walked

… on the beach we …

- [x] went
- [ ] have gone
- [ ] had gone

… home.

c The shop …

- [ ] hasn't been open
- [x] wasn't open
- [ ] wasn't opening

… on Sunday.

d We …

- [x] were shopping
- [ ] have been shopping
- [ ] had shopped

… all day last Saturday.

e They …

- [ ] were playing
- [ ] played
- [x] have played

… music together for two years now.

f Up to now we …

- [ ] were
- [ ] were being
- [x] have been

… here for a week.

g Joe …

- [ ] was surfing
- [x] has been surfing
- [ ] had surfed

… since he was young.

h They …

- [ ] were driving
- [ ] drove
- [x] had driven

… a long way before they saw the sea.

i In Hollywood Tom …

- [ ] has been imagining
- [ ] was imagining
- [x] imagined

… himself as a film star.

j Three weeks ago I …

- [ ] have been walking
- [ ] had walked
- [x] was walking

… along this street in the rain.

Topic 3: What's planned?

16

		true	false	not in the text
a	Sam is going to go to America with his friend, Becky.	☐	☑	☐
b	Becky thinks the holiday will be expensive.	☐	☐	☑
c	The holiday is for twenty-one days.	☑	☐	☐
d	Sam is flying at the start of the month.	☑	☐	☐
e	He is going to stay in some nice hotels.	☐	☐	☑
f	He is not flying from Germany.	☑	☐	☐
g	Sam is going to take books and magazines with him.	☐	☑	☐
h	When Becky flew, there was a bad storm.	☐	☐	☑
i	Sam's friend has been on a long flight, too.	☑	☐	☐
j	She couldn't sleep on the plane.	☐	☑	☐

17
- a They **are collecting** their new car tomorrow.
- b On Wednesday I **am going to watch** a film at the cinema.
- c "Are you going into town? **I'll walk** with you."
- d The train **arrives** at 16.30 this afternoon.
- e I **am going to buy** a book this afternoon for Kim.
- f It **will snow** soon.
- g School **starts** half an hour later tomorrow.
- h I expect we **will be** early.
- i You've bought a big picture. Where **are you going to put** it?
- j They **will probably be** on the next train.

18

sign	meaning	German
nightly	every night	*jeden Abend / jede Nacht*
inclement	bad	*rau*
high	(here) strong	*stark / kräftig*
performance	(concert / theatre) show	*Darstellung / Aufführung*
stroller	something to push small children in (BE pushchair / buggy)	*Kinderwagen*
permitted	allowed	*erlaubt/gestattet*

19 *(example answer)*

Hi Carol,

I'm going to see "The Sirens of TI" tomorrow night. The performance starts at 8.30 p.m. I hope the weather'll stay nice, because otherwise they'll cancel the show. I expect it'll be lots of fun. My little brother has to walk because small children in strollers are not permitted. We're travelling home on Sunday.

See you soon,

Amanda

20

a We **are going** to the concert in New York at the weekend. The tickets were quite expensive.
b I think **you will enjoy** your holiday.
c My TV programme **finishes** in half an hour.
d What are your plans? **Are you going** swimming tonight?
e **We are going** by train tomorrow, I've got the tickets already.
f It **will be** dark by 6 o'clock tonight.
g "I **will repair** my bike later," she answered quickly.
h It **is going to be** a super party, Jane has been planning it all week.
i You said that you would phone on Tuesday but when **will you phone**?
j We **won't arrive** until 9 p.m. because of the bus.
k "Decide now!" Kevin said angrily. "**Will you help** me or not?"
l I **am driving** to the Lake District at the weekend to visit my parents.
m The plane **lands** at 5 o'clock tomorrow.
n I'm sure I **won't sleep** very well tonight.
o We **are going to have** a barbecue tonight.

a	will go	**are going**	are going to go
b	you are going to enjoy	**you will enjoy**	you are enjoying
c	**finishes**	will finish	is finishing
d	Will you go	Do you go	**Are you going**
e	**We are going**	We go	We will go
f	goes	is going to be	**will be**
g	**will repair**	am repairing	am going to repair
h	will be	**is going to be**	be
i	are you phoning	phone	**will you phone**

j	aren't arriving	**won't arrive**	aren't going to arrive
k	Help	**Will you help**	Are you going to help
l	**am driving**	drive	will drive
m	will land	is going to land	**lands**
n	am not going to sleep	**won't sleep**	am not sleeping
o	**are going to have**	will have	have

Topic 4: Hollywood

21 a Cindy and Jim went to Venice Beach and Hollywood on the same day.

This statement is ☐ true
☑ false

because **they went to Hollywood the next day**. / … **the next day Cindy asked how to get to Hollywood**.

b **If they drove / If they went by car**, they would need about half an hour.

c If you walk along Hollywood Boulevard, what can you see?

A ☐

B ☐

C ☑

d The photo was taken in Hollywood Boulevard and the people in it are making a film. / … where a film is being made. /
The photo was taken outside Mann's Chinese Theatre. It shows people making a film. / It shows a film crew at work.

e In which building are the Oscars given?

A ☐

B ☑

C ☐

f Jim thinks Hollywood is interesting but he doesn't find it very attractive. / ... but he doesn't like it.

g Which house does Cindy probably see?

A ☐

B ☐

C ☑

h If you were a film star, where would you go shopping?

A ☐

B ☐

C ☑

i Because there are no prices (in the shop windows).

22
- **a** If we park here, we can walk to the theatre.
- **b** If we lived here, we could go shopping in Rodeo Drive.
- **c** If I lived in Beverly Hills, I would need a lot of money.
- **d** If I had a Walk of Fame star, I would want it over there.
- **e** If we go inside the Kodak Theatre, we can see where the Oscars happen.
- **f** We will be in a film if we stand here.
- **g** We can take photos of the Hollywood sign if we drive along this road.

23
- **a** If it is sunny tomorrow, we will go / can go to the beach.
- **b** If you are hungry, buy something to eat.
- **c** If he flew, it would be / could be expensive.
- **d** If you liked rock music, you could listen / would listen to this band.
- **e** If the hotel is nice, they will recommend it to their friends.
- **f** If we eat now, we won't / will not need anything later.
- **g** If I saw someone famous, I would ask for an autograph.

24
- **a** If I **had acted** in the film, I **would have won / might have won** an Oscar.
- **b** If I **had stood** on the wall, I **would have seen / could have seen** them making the film.
- **c** If he **had lived** in America, he **would have spoken** English.
- **d** If my computer **hadn't broken down**, I **would have finished** writing about Hollywood.
- **e** If we **had gone** by bus, we **could have got off / would have got off** outside the theatre.

25
- **a** If our football team had won, I would have celebrated.
- **b** If Julia's train had been late, she would have missed the bus.
- **c** If the sea had been warm, we could have swum in it. / If the sea hadn't been so cold, …
- **d** If I had lost / hadn't found my camera, I couldn't have taken a lot of photos of you.
- **e** If she hadn't been ill, we wouldn't have stayed at home. / If she had been well, …

26

1	2	3	4	5	6	7
D	E	G	F	A	C	B

27 *Tourist:* Excuse me, do you know how much the car park costs?
You: **Yes, I do. It's $ 1 for every hour between 8.00 a.m. and 6.00 p.m.**
Tourist: Where do I have to pay?
You: **You have to pay at the pay station.**
Tourist: How do I get a ticket?
You: **You press any key, enter your parking space number, put the correct money into the machine, for example $ 2 for two hours, and then you press OK.**
Tourist: What do I do with the ticket?
You: **You keep it./You don't have to put it in your car, (... so you can keep it).**
Tourist: What happens if I have a problem with the parking meter at the pay station?
You: **There is someone (who) you can phone. / You can phone the number on the sign./You phone 310 285 2467.**

28 *(example answer)*
If I went to America, I would like to visit New York. I think New York would be very exciting. I would like to see Manhattan and then visit the Statue of Liberty. I would also take some extra money with me so that I could go shopping there and buy something special. And if I was in New York for a few days, I would go to a Broadway show one evening.

29
- **a** Photo **E**: If I **had visited** the Redwood Groves, I **would have turned** right.
- **b** Photo **B**: If I **had gone to** Malibu, I **would have seen** 27 miles of scenic beauty.
- **c** Photo **C**: If I **had driven** east, I **would have been** on Route 66.
- **d** Photo **D**: If I **had been** on the tribal roads, I **couldn't have jogged/ wouldn't have jogged**.
- **e** Photo **A**: If we **had stayed** here, we **could have bought/would have bought** a pizza.

30

a	If it had rained, I …	☐ won't go ☑ wouldn't have gone ☐ went	… for a walk.
b	If we stay in this hotel, it …	☐ was ☑ will be ☐ might have been	… cheaper than the last one.
c	If she goes by car, she	☐ will find ☐ wouldn't have to find ☑ may not find	… anywhere to park.
d	If Jim hadn't seen me, he …	☐ will phone ☐ would phone ☑ would have phoned	… me.
e	If we looked out of our window, we …	☑ could see ☐ can see ☐ could have seen	… the Hollywood sign.
f	If we had walked, we …	☐ will be ☐ would be ☑ would have been	… here sooner.
g	If you go to Hollywood, you …	☐ shall visit ☑ should visit ☐ should have visited	… Beverly Hills, too.

Topic 5: The park ranger

31 **a** Yosemite / Yellowstone / the Statue of Liberty

b What isn't a ranger's job?

A ☐

B ☐

C ☑

c Catlin's aim was to stop Americans destroying their beautiful countryside and losing parts of their culture. / ... was to look after some specific areas.

d The state parks were protected but there was no one to look after them. / The ranger service was necessary to look after the parks.

e What can some rangers do?

A ☐

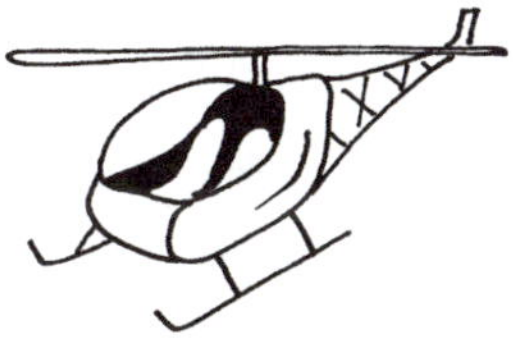

B ☑

C ☐

f In a ranger's car you can find special equipment to deal with many different types of problems, brochures and maps.

g You can phone 0924/456/6729 or look on the website www.nps.gov.

32 **a** So do we.
b So might Jane.
c Jason is, too.
d So does Fabian.
e So do I.
f Gina does, too.

33 **a** Neither does Martin.
b Neither do I.
c Nor is Lucy.
d Nor can we.
e Linda couldn't either.
f He wouldn't either.
g Jane and Tom don't either.

34 **a** Mike likes art. So does Kylie.
b I don't feed the animals. Neither / Nor does Harry. / Harry doesn't either.
c We enjoyed the view. So did my parents. / My parents did, too.
d She hasn't been to the concert. Neither / Nor have I. / I haven't either.
e John has got a skateboard. So have I. / I have, too.

35

job	picture	German translation
builder	d	*Bauarbeiter(in)*
electrician	f	*Elektriker(in)*
engineer	b	*Ingenieur(in)*
flight attendant	a	*Flugbegleiter(in)*
hairdresser	h	*Friseur(in)*
mechanic	g	*Mechaniker(in)*
nurse	c	*Krankenschwester / Krankenpfleger*
shop assistant / sales assistant	e	*Verkäufer(in)*

36 Check your answers with a dictionary or on the internet. You can also ask your teacher.

37 *(example answer)*
Name: Alena Fischer
Address: Zugspitzstr. 10,
45468 Mühlheim, Germany
Tel: +49 (0)208/98765
E-mail: a.fischer@t.com
Job: vet's assistant

Why do you want this job? Answer in 30 – 50 words.
I like animals and I think I would be very good working with them. I like the idea of helping them to get better and also making their owners happy. I also like meeting people and talking to them. At school I enjoyed Biology and this might be useful. *(49 words)*

Write a profile about yourself. Write at least 50 words.
I am 15 years old and have got many friends and interests. I like animals and I help in an animal home at the weekends. My family also has a dog, Charlie, but I am responsible for him, so I go for walks, feed him and take him to the vet. In my free time, I play tennis and handball, too. I listen to music and enjoy reading. *(68 words)*

38
- **a** I enjoy my job. So does my friend Pete.
- **b** Greg is from America. So are Peter and Jane. / Peter and Jane are, too.
- **c** My brother can't swim. Neither / Nor can my sister. / My sister can't swim either.
  My brother doesn't swim. Neither / Nor does my sister. / My sister doesn't swim either.
- **d** Harry drives a lot. So do Mr and Mrs Smith. / Mr and Mrs Smith do, too.
- **e** Tricia doesn't like very hot weather. Neither / Nor do many people. / Many people don't either.
- **f** I can work outside. So can Kim. / Kim can, too.
- **g** My dogs are big. So are yours. / Yours are, too.
- **h** We didn't buy a house. Neither / Nor did our friends. / Our friends didn't either.
  We aren't going to buy a house. Neither / Nor are our friends. / Our friends aren't either.
- **i** My parents are playing tennis tonight. So am I. / I am, too.
- **j** I am never sad. Neither / Nor is my wife. / My wife isn't either.
- **k** I haven't been to New York yet. Neither / Nor has my daughter. / My daughter hasn't either.

Topic 6: Changing the world

39

date	who	invention	photo
1899	Johan Vaaler	(the) paper clip	H
1973	Martin Cooper	(the) mobile phone	D
2001	Vinnie Chieco	the name 'iPod'	G
2004	Mark Zuckerberg	Facebook	A

40

		true	false	not given
a	Zuckerberg was studying technology at Harvard University. **Not given because Zuckerberg was at Harvard University but the text doesn't say what he was studying.**	☐	☐	✓
b	Students didn't like networking. **False because the website was very successful with the students.**	☐	✓	☐
c	One invention was tested outside.	✓	☐	☐
d	The size is still the main problem of Cooper's idea. **False because mobile phones are now small and light.**	☐	✓	☐
e	Chieco invented the iPod. **False because he only invented the name.**	☐	✓	☐
f	Online music stores are very successful. **Not given because it only says that the online stores were developed.**	☐	☐	✓
g	Vaaler's invention is still in its original form.	✓	☐	☐
h	Before 1835 pins were used to hold pieces of paper together. **False because pins were not invented until 1835.**	☐	✓	☐

41
- **a** A successful website was started by Mark Zuckerberg.
- **b** Websites will be made even more interesting (by new technology).
- **c** Many people in New York were shocked by Martin Cooper.
- **d** The iPod was introduced (by him).
- **e** The name 'iPod' was invented by Vinnie Chieco.
- **f** An online music store was developed.
- **g** My presentation will be improved.
- **h** Her paper clips have been used.

42
- **a** A map **is being read**.
- **b** A new shop **is being built**.
- **c** The view **is being looked at / enjoyed** by many visitors.
- **d** Yesterday, music **was being played**.
- **e** Last week, newspapers **were being sold** in the street.
- **f** The car **isn't being driven** on a normal road.

43

German	English
teilweise	partly
häufig	frequently
völlig	completely
selten	seldom
oft	often
gelegentlich	occasionally

44
- **a** The question was partly answered by Jason.
- **b** Sport is frequently / often played (by young people).
- **c** The castle is occasionally / seldom opened.
- **d** Text messages are frequently sent.
- **e** The car was seldom driven (by the man).
- **f** Jane's work was completely done by Jane herself.

45 The first flight was made in 1903. The plane was called 'The Flyer'. It was flown by the Wright brothers. The first flight was completed by Orville Wright. Four flights were made that day. On the fourth flight, the plane was flown for 260 metres by Orville's brother.

46 **a** Today, it **is visited** by millions of people around the world. (Zuckerberg)
b Cooper's invention **is carried** by most people today ... (Cooper)
c An online music store **was** also **developed** so that this product could work. (Chieco)
d ... and it **hasn't been changed**./In 1835, pins **were invented** for this ... (Vaaler)

47 **a** Her mobile phone is being repaired.
b PCs had been used for many years before laptops.
c A new computer programme will be developed.
d My camera is being used by Tom and Mike.
e The cars were being driven very fast.
f A lot of books were being carried to the library.
g She has been seen in the park.
h E-mails were being sent to parents.
i The first cars were built a long time ago.
j Chatting on the internet is enjoyed by many young people.
k The new car design was liked (by the company).
l The house was being painted all day (by Jason).
m A film about school has been made by the pupils.

Topic 7: Living with languages

48 **a** No, it isn't./no, it isn't
b to communicate with in business
c No, it isn't. /no, it isn't
d (some) spelling and expressions
e (because) it's a living language
f handy
g a German word that looks and sounds like an English one but with a different meaning
h Angst/Schadenfreude
i in the Indian communities in Britain/... on signs
j No, it isn't. /no, it isn't
k Wales

49

a

Photo: **8**	Shopping in some parts of British towns.
Text: **In the Indian communities in Britain you can often see examples of this on signs.**	

b

Photo: **5**	Walking along an American street
Text: **What you may not know is that the two countries also have some different expressions: …**	

c

Photo: **1**	A business meeting in India
Text: **However, it is English that has become the language used to communicate with in business in most countries around the world … / English is also used in India …**	

d

Photo: **9**	This can't be correct, can it?
Text: **And sometimes you will even see signs with mistakes on them!**	

e

Photo: **3**	A sign in a street in Wales
Text: **If you look at Wales, for example, you will see that another language is often used there, too.**	

50

a ❶ I was told a story.
❷ A story was told to me.

b She was bought a new mobile phone.

c ❶ Tim was sent an e-mail.
❷ An e-mail was sent to Tim.

d ❶ They were taken some pieces of cake.
❷ Some pieces of cake were taken to them.

e Janet's bike was stolen at the supermarket.

f ❶ The children were shown the website.
❷ The website was shown to the children.

g ❶ We were lent the money.
❷ The money was lent to us.

h ❶ She was given the book.
❷ The book was given to her.

i The film about Africa was watched.

51
- **a** The view is being looked at.
- **b** The concert was listened to (by many people).
- **c** The bridge was being driven across.
- **d** Flying is known to be very safe.
- **e** Surfing is said to be difficult.
- **f** English is believed to be an important language to learn.
- **g** Sweets can be bought at the shop.
- **h** The trees in the park may be climbed.
- **i** The road shouldn't be run across.

52 Before I flew to America, I **had been told** by friends that some English words were different there. When I arrived, I hired a car. Driving an American car **was said to be** easy but some signs **could be** difficult for English people to understand.

I found one – '*Ped xing*'. I sent a photo and a text message to a friend. "This sign **can be seen** everywhere," I wrote. "What does it mean?" My friend wasn't sure so he asked a lot of people for their opinion, too. Two days later I got an answer, "... it **is thought to mean** 'pedestrian crossing'."

I had a problem with my car one day, too. An American stopped and helped me. A few phone calls **were made** and suddenly my 'problem' became an 'issue'! But my issue **was dealt with** very quickly and so I was happy again.

53
- **a** The animals mustn't be fed.
- **b** The roller coaster is thought to be scary.
- **c** The car's wheels have been taken off.
- **d** The Hollywood Bowl is said to be famous.

54 **a**

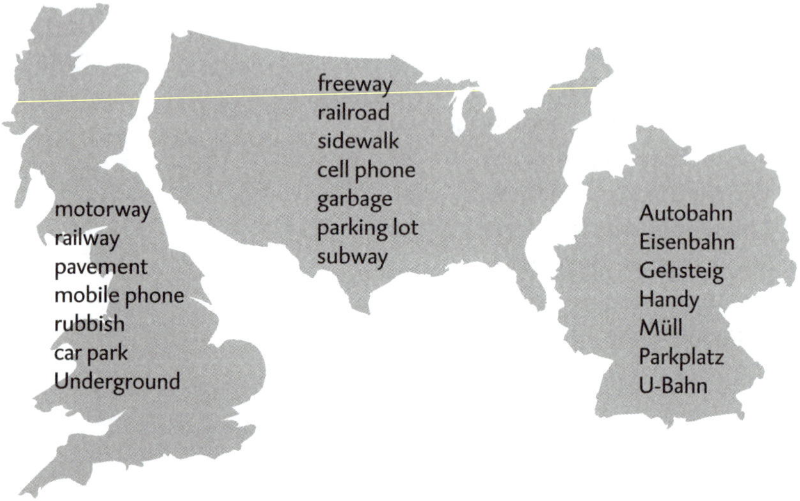

b from Britain: photo 2 (Underground), photo 6 (car park)
from America: photo 1 (cell phone), photo 3 (sidewalks), photo 4 (railroad)
can't say: photo 5

55 **British English:**
Chris and Mandy took **the Underground** to **the railway** station. Yesterday, their car **had been parked** in **the car park** there by their parents. At the station they walked along **the pavement** until they came to it. They got into their car and then **drove** to **the motorway**. The roads **are thought to be** busy on Saturdays but this one wasn't. Mandy's **mobile phone** didn't work because the battery was empty so their parents **couldn't be phoned** on the way home.

American English:
Chris and Mandy took **the subway** to **the railroad** station. Yesterday, their car **had been parked** in **the parking lot** there by their parents. At the station they walked along **the sidewalk** until they came to it. They got into their car and then **drove** to **the freeway**. The roads **are thought to be** busy on Saturdays but this one wasn't. Mandy's **cell phone** didn't work because the battery was empty so their parents **couldn't be phoned** on the way home.

56
a He was given a nice present. / A nice present was given to him.
b The picture is being looked at (by Tom).
c The film is believed to be a true story.
d The grass can be walked on.
e The house was broken into.
f Peter must be phoned later.
g This pop group is said to be very good.
h Driving is thought to be easier than flying.

Topic 8: Sport and leisure

57 **a** Where was the information about Trafalgar Sports?

A ☐

B ☑

C ☐

b The open days are …

- ☐ next weekend.
- ☐ during the week.
- ☑ at a weekend.

c What is Justine going to do first?

A ☐

B ☐

C ☑

d
- *indoor sports:* squash, badminton, fitness studio
- *outdoor sports:* go-karting, mountain biking, sailing, windsurfing, golf
- *both:* climbing, tennis, horse riding, swimming

e 13 hours

f 2 hours

g 3 (phone, e-mail, website)

h Which sport can't you do at Trafalgar Sports?

A ☐

B ☑

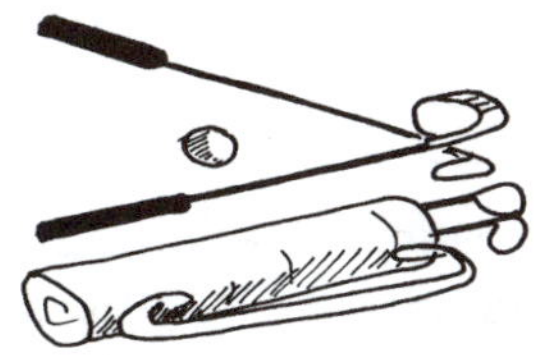

C ☐

58
- **a** Manny says (that) Justine has just finished reading the advert.
- **b** Jason told Chang (that) Martin had run to the shop.
- **c** Owen wrote (that) he had been swimming.
- **d** Tina writes (that) they were playing golf.
- **e** Martin said (that) he was in the garden.
- **f** Rachel tells Mike (that) Trevor has gone home.
- **g** Arthur said (that) Carol loved horses.

59
- **a** Justine writes (that) she likes horse riding.
- **b** Chang answers (that) he prefers go-karting because it is more fun.
- **c** Suki told Geoff (that) Carol's mum played golf there.
- **d** Harry said (that) he had been to the sports centre already.
- **e** Maria wrote (that) they had gone the week before, too, and it had been really nice.
- **f** Leo explained (that) he hadn't booked a course yet.
- **g** Justine says (that) she saw the advert and she wants Chang to go with her.
- **h** Chang tells Justine (that) he can't go at the weekend.
- **i** Suki tells everyone (that) she phoned the sports centre and booked a windsurfing course.

60
- **a** Justine wrote (that) she would like to go to the sports centre.
  She said (that) she would play badminton.
  She explained (that) she might go mountain biking, too.
  She told Chang (that) she could swim so she might also take a windsurfing course.
- **b** Chang explained (that) he couldn't go on Saturday.
  He said (that) he had to help his mum.
  He told Justine (that) he could go on Sunday.
  He suggested (that) she could phone him later.
  He wrote (that) he might ask his mum again if he could go.

61

happy	↔	**unhappy**
perfect	↔	**imperfect**
agree	↔	**disagree**
clear	↔	**unclear**
possible	↔	**impossible**
advantage	↔	**disadvantage**
legal	↔	**illegal**

62
- **a** The children were very immature.
- **b** The bridge was unsafe.
- **c** The man disconnected the electricity.
- **d** The question was illogical.

63 Justine's mum explained (**that**) **they had decided to go/she had decided to take her daughter and her daughter's friends** to an open day. She then told him that everyone **had jumped into the car and they had driven away** but then the car **had suddenly stopped**. She explained that **everyone had got out of the car and had pushed it to the side of the road**. They **had been lucky because there had been somewhere** to park. She told the policeman there **was water on the road and it was coming from their car** and that she **had phoned** a garage on her mobile.

64
- **a** Tricia said (**that**) **they had to learn to swim**.
- **b** Tony told Mike (**that**) **there was a new sports centre**.
- **c** Mrs Jones said (**that**) **she might wash the car**.
- **d** Jason wrote (**that**) **Jan was playing tennis**.
- **e** Melissa answered (**that**) **she knew because she had just seen Jan at the sports centre**.
- **f** Mr Smith said (**that**) **he would read the newspaper but he couldn't find it**.

65 Kim wrote (**that**) **she was having a rest** because **she had just been riding her mountain bike**. She said **she had been along some great tracks**. She told Mark (**that**) **some were easy and others were (really) hard** and (**that**) **there was a river to cross without a bridge**. She complained (**that**) **she was very wet**. She suggested (**that**) **he met her/they met at the café in 10 minutes/10 minutes later**.

Topic 9: Hungry?

66 **a** England/jacket potato
b Wash it so that the skin is clean.
c to put holes into the potato
d between 10 – 15 minutes
e
- (large) potato
- tin of tuna
- (cheddar or Gouda) cheese
- mayonnaise

f
- cheddar cheese
- fresh prawns

g

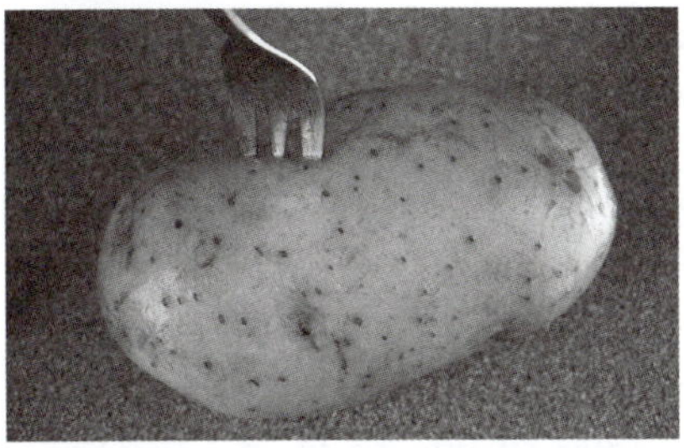

1 Put some small holes into the potato with a fork.

4 I often have prawns …

3 … grate some cheese.

2 … into the microwave at full power …

67 a
- Anna thanks Peter for **his** recipe.
- Peter thinks (**that**) **she/Anna will like it**.
- Anna says (**that**) **she is sure she will**.

b
- Marcia says (**that**) **they are coming to their/his party**.
- Tom replies (**that**) **he will see her/them later**.

c
- Harry told Noah (**that**) **his mum wanted him to go to the shop for her**.
- Noah replied (**that**) **he could come/go with them. They were going to the shop, too**.

d
- Gina told Sammy (**that**) **their new neighbours were very nice**.
- Sammy said (**that**) **he had spoken to them already**.

68
- a Ntila explained (that) she lived in Kenya and the day before they hadn't had anything to eat.
- b She said (that) every morning there they collected water before going to school.
- c She complained (that) that day she hadn't had any breakfast.
- d She told Jack (that) the week before their goat had died.
- e She said (that) that was a big problem for their family.
- f Jack told Ntila (that) he lived in Britain and (that) they never had any problems with food there.
- g He said (that) he had been hungry the day before.
- h He explained (that) his mum had gone shopping the Friday before/ last Friday.
- i He said (that) the next day they were going to a nice restaurant.
- j He explained to Ntila (that) that day they were having fish and chips for dinner.

69
- a Jack wanted to know how many people were in her/their family.
- b Jack asked if she had to walk to school.
- c Jack wondered what they/she ate.
- d Jack asked where she collected the water from.
- e Jack wanted to know why her family didn't buy a new goat.
- f Jack asked whether/if she had a bike.
- g Jack wanted to know if/whether it was warm where she lived.
- h Jack asked if/whether she lived in a village.
- i Jack wondered who looked after the animals.
- j Jack asked when she went to school.

k Ntila asked if/whether he lived in a big city.
l Ntila wanted to know why he had been hungry the day before.
m Ntila asked if/whether there were a lot of shops near his/their house.
n Ntila wondered what a restaurant was. She explained that they didn't have any.
o Ntila wanted to know when he/they ate.

70

sign	1	2	3	4	5	6	7	8
statement	g	c	d	b	a	h	f	e

a Arthur told the boys **to put their rubbish in the bin**.
b Fiona told her daughter **to wait for the school bus there**.
c The hotel owner asked guests **not to smoke near the door**.
d The policemen advised the old people **to use the crossing**.
e The sign asks visitors **not to go there**.
f The national park warned people **to look out for pumas**.
g Tom tells Peter **not to walk there at night**.
h The Navajo Council orders people **not to park there**.

71

microwave – ***in der Mikrowelle erwärmen***

bake – ***backen***

grill – ***grillen***

roast – ***rösten/braten***

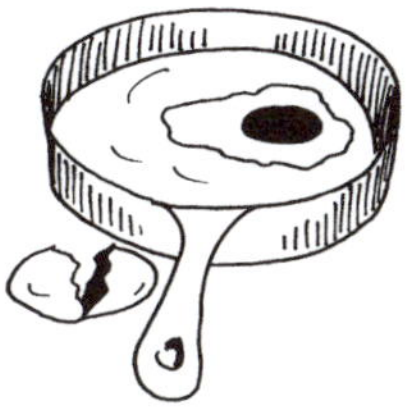

fry – ***braten***

boil – ***kochen***

72
- **a** My aunt would roast a chicken.
- **b** Grandma would bake a cake.
- **c** My mum would fry the fish.
- **d** I would fry/boil the egg.
- **e** My sister would grill a beefburger.
- **f** My dad would boil the carrots.
- **g** My brother would microwave a ready-made meal.

73 **Toast Hawaii:**

Toast two pieces of bread. Put some ham on the toast and then some pineapple on top of the ham. After that grate some cheese and put this on top of the ham and the pineapple. Finally, grill everything for a few minutes.

English breakfast:

Fry two eggs and the sausages. Grill three pieces of bacon and toast two slices of bread. You must turn the bacon over so that both sides are grilled.

74
- **a** Bob asked Julia if/whether she had bought a new car.
- **b** Kim said (that) that was her sister and she was staying with her until the next day.
- **c** Andrew explained (that) he was looking for his coat because he had lost it.
- **d** Thomas wanted to know how to make spaghetti bolognese./ Thomas wanted to know how they made spaghetti bolognese.
- **e** Carol told Sue (that) the week before they had gone to a nice restaurant.
- **f** Jenny asks Mike to post the letter for her.
- **g** Linda advised the children not to swim in the cold river that day.
- **h** Mr and Mrs Fielder explain to Jason (that) they haven't visited their friends in America for a long time.
- **i** Sammy wanted to know whose shoes those were.

Topic 10: What is Art?

			true	false	not in the text
75	a	The pupils have work to do after their visit. **True because they have to write about some things that they looked at.**	✓		
	b	The exhibition was in Trafalgar Square. **False because the exhibition was at the Tate Modern in London.**		✓	
	c	Nelson was a soldier at Trafalgar. **False because Nelson was a captain on a boat.**		✓	
	d	Nelson's boat is very famous. **Not in the text because Zita only says that Nelson maybe had a boat like the galleon in Trafalgar Square.**			✓
	e	Pippa expected the box to drop on her. **True because when she walked under it she thought it would fall on top of her.**	✓		
	f	Everyone could climb into the box. **False because there was a ramp into the box, therefore you could walk into it.**		✓	
	g	Pippa took a light with her. **Not in the text because she doesn't mention having a light.**			✓
	h	Pippa decided to explore the inside of the box. **True because she walked into it.**	✓		
	i	You could walk through the box. **False because Pippa came to the end wall and turned around, therefore she couldn't walk 'through' the box – only in it.**		✓	
	j	There were a lot of accidents. **False because people going out of the box could see the people coming into it and miss them.**		✓	

76

A ☑

B ☐

C ☐

D ☑

77

- **a** Most people know **how to use** the internet.
- **b** Pippa explained **where to find / how to find** the information.
- **c** James asked her **who to phone / when to phone**.
- **d** Eric didn't know **where to go** in London.
- **e** The teacher told us **where to meet / when to meet**.
- **f** Do you know **how to paint / what to paint**?
- **g** Peter never knows **what to write** about.

78

I wanted **to go** to the Tate Modern but my teacher told me **to go** to Trafalgar Square and **(to) write** about the art work there. I remembered **to take** my camera with me so I **took** some interesting pictures. *Zita, 9 B 2*

I would love **to visit** London again. I don't **know** how people can afford **to live** there though. Everything **is** really expensive. Our teacher warned us **to be** careful with our money there. He advised us **not to put / carry** our money in our back pockets of our jeans. We remembered **to do** that! *Eric, 9 B 2*

It's easy to learn **(how) to use** the Underground or the buses. I **found** my way from one place to another with a street map. Some tourists even asked me **to help** them! It **was** only because I **had** a map. *Pippa, 9 B 2*

79 **a** Eric's grandad … a painter.

- [x] used to *be* (*be*)
- [ ] is used to ______ (*be*)

b The 9th class … interesting projects; they have done many of them already.

- [ ] used to ______ (*do*)
- [x] are used to *doing* (*do*)

c Pippa … lots of photographs but she has now stopped.

- [x] used to *take* (*take*)
- [ ] is used to ______ (*take*)

d Mr and Mrs Johnson … on the floor – their backs hurt.

- [ ] used to ______ (*work*)
- [x] aren't used to *working* (*work*)

e Michael and Johnny … to school but now they go by bus.

- [x] used to ______ (*cycle*)
- [ ] are used to ______ (*cycle*)

f Steffie … the piano at the school fair but this year she is helping us.

- [x] used to *play* (*play*)
- [ ] is used to ______ (*play*)

g The school fair … on a Saturday.

- [x] used to *be* (*be*)
- [ ] was used to ______ (*be*)

h Everyone … a fun time at the school fair in the summer.

- [ ] used to ______ (*have*)
- [x] is used to *having* (*have*)

i After the project everyone has to help to tidy up but they … that.

- [ ] used to
- [x] are used to

j Gina complained of a bad back; she … the hard work!

- [ ] used to
- [x] isn't used to

80 a The paper **to use** is here.
b If you want something **to cut** the paper with, it's on the table.
c The string **to tie** things with is next to the scissors.
d There is a lot of work **to do / to be done**, so please help.
e The objects **to wrap / to be wrapped** are on the tables but we have to start with the walls and the floor.
f We have put the information **to read** about the project on the door.
g The chair is too difficult for me **to wrap.**
h My fingers are too big **to tie** the string.
i Have you got enough paper **to cover** the whole room?
j It's easier **to begin / to start** with the legs of the table.
k The hardest thing **to do** was the backboard.

81 a non-stop / ununterbrochen
b
- *(the) use:* Verwendung / Nutzung / Gebrauch
- *(to) use:* benutzen
- *used to:* was man in der Vergangenheit regelmäßig gemacht hat, aber jetzt nicht mehr tut
- *(to) be used to:* an etwas gewöhnt sein

c plinth
d One and Other/Antony Gormley
e in the morning
f 1 hour (2,400 divided by 100 days = 24 people each day = 1 person per hour)

82 *(example answer)*
Dear Mr Gormley,
I would like to take part in your art project in Trafalgar Square. I want to do this because I think it would be fun to be part of a work of art. We have also talked about modern art at school and I want to know more about what it means. From the top of the plinth I think there will be a fantastic view and I can watch what everyone is doing below me. I would like to stand on top of the plinth at midday because it is very busy in Trafalgar Square at that time and there is always a lot to see, and I can listen to Big Ben, too.
Kind regards,
(your first and last name) *(120 words)*

83
- **a** Do you know where **to buy** Mike a present?
- **b** I don't know who **to phone** about my car.
- **c** Is there anything interesting **to see** in London?
- **d** Linda would like **to visit** Manchester.
- **e** Is it quicker **to drive**?
- **f** Can I ask John **to help** me tomorrow?
- **g** Sally asked Mike how **to repair** her bike.

84
- **a** Sally says it's too early **to go** swimming.
- **b** Harry can't afford **to fly** to New York.
- **c** Mum's car **is getting** dirtier and dirtier every day.
- **d** The T-shirt **to buy** is the red one.
- **e** I would have **expected** nicer weather.
- **f** I would love **to have** a dog.
- **g** Sally expected **not to win** the race.
- **h** The journey **was / is** longer than I **remembered** it.
- **i** Larry's garden was big enough **to play** football in.
- **j** I had hoped **to learn** French when I **went** to Paris.
- **k** We remembered **to close / closing** all the windows before we left.
- **l** The boys were told **not to walk** on the grass.
- **m** Anna **drives / drove** to work but she prefers **to cycle / cycling** there.
- **n** The man **closed** the door and then began **to read / reading** his book.
- **o** Jason wanted to know how **not to get** the carpet dirty when he **painted** the wall.

Topic 11: The Grand Canyon

85

Paragraph	Heading
A	*No small place*
B	*River facts*
C	*Exploring the river*
D	*Looking after yourself*

86

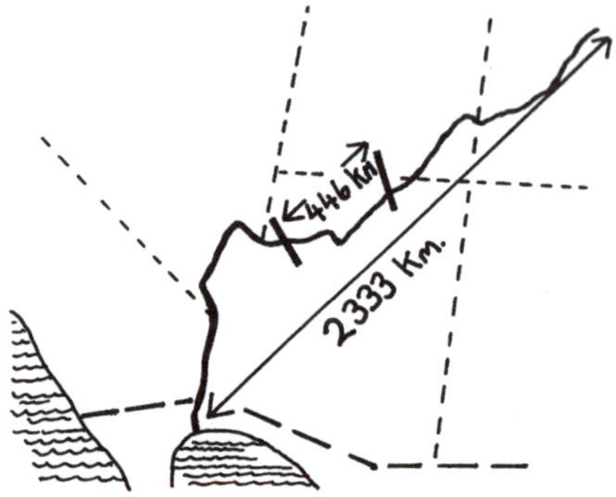

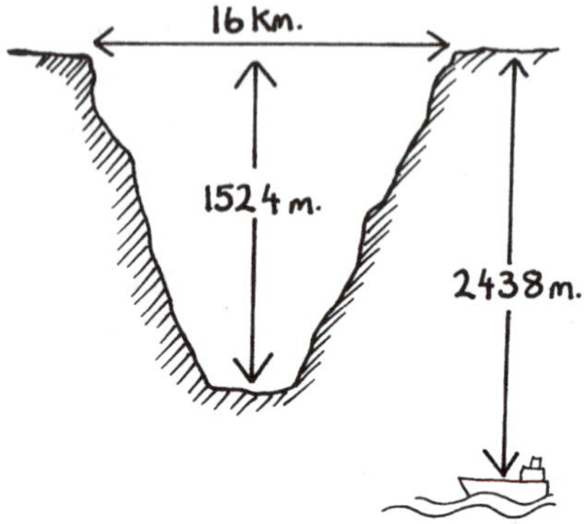

87
- **a** because the air is thin and it is hot / because of (the) thin air and (the) heat
- **b** there was no map to follow / (they had) no map
- **c** 24 days
- **d** 6 hours
- **e** 4 litres
- **f** before 10 a.m. and after 4 p.m.

88
- **a** I can't imagine **living** in that house over there.
- **b** **Cycling / Mountain biking** is allowed in the Grand Canyon National Park.
- **c** **Walking / Hiking** when it is hot is dangerous.
- **d** Most old people can only stand **sitting** in the sunshine a short time.
- **e** **Flying** through the Grand Canyon is possible.
- **f** **Feeding** the animals is not allowed.
- **g** Many people enjoy **eating** in the restaurant.
- **h** I suggest **waiting** for the bus here.
- **i** We enjoyed **looking** at the view.

89
- **a** I apologise for **being** late.
- **b** Before **leaving** the house I **read** the newspaper.
- **c** Yesterday I **drove** to the cinema.
- **d** Instead of **cycling** I **went** by bus last night.
- **e** I **wrote** some e-mails while **travelling** on the train.
- **f** Do you often **jog** in the park?
- **g** Do you worry about **walking** where there **are** snakes?
- **h** It's not worth **phoning** Toni tonight; she **is / will be** at a party.
- **i** After **visiting** the Grand Canyon we **stayed** in Las Vegas.
- **j** Charlie said he would **speak** to Sam after **talking** to Amanda.

90
- **a** The bus driver continued **driving/to drive** along the road.
- **b** I would like **to visit** the Grand Canyon.
- **c** Pam would prefer **to fly** to New York.
- **d** We loved **looking at/to look at** the fantastic views.
- **e** We have just begun **washing/to wash** the car.
- **f** They hated **travelling/to travel** a long way.
- **g** She would love **to watch** the film.

91
- **a** Paula remembered to send Zoe an e-mail.
  - ☑ Paula did not forget to send Zoe an e-mail.
  - ☐ Paula can remember that she sent Zoe an e-mail.
- **b** George remembers flying to America.
  - ☐ George has to fly to America.
  - ☑ George can remember when he flew to America.
- **c** We stopped buying newspapers a few weeks ago.
  - ☑ We have not bought any newspapers for a few weeks now.
  - ☐ A few weeks ago we bought some newspapers.
- **d** Tom stopped to look into a shop's window.
  - ☐ Tom used to look into a shop's window but he now doesn't.
  - ☑ Tom stopped and then looked into a shop's window.
- **e** Lucy always forgets to take her camera with her.
  - ☐ Lucy can never remember that she has got her camera with her.
  - ☑ Lucy's camera is at home.
- **f** I forgot buying this T-shirt.
  - ☐ I should have bought the T-shirt but I didn't.
  - ☑ I have just found this T-shirt that I had bought.
- **g** They remember to meet Larry at the hotel.
  - ☐ They have met Larry before and can remember him.
  - ☑ They haven't forgotten that they will meet Larry.
- **h** She stopped e-mailing Mike years ago.
  - ☑ She often e-mailed Mike a long time ago but doesn't any more.
  - ☐ When she was e-mailing Mike, she had to stop.

92
- a **Hiking / Walking** in summer in the Grand Canyon
- b Instead of **suffering** hike smart.
- c When walking a long way start **drinking / to drink plenty of water** and electrolyte drinks.
- d **Eating carbohydrates** and **salty foods** is necessary.
- e Remember **to hike / to walk during the cooler parts of the day**.
- f **Going slowly** and **resting often** can save your life.
- g Don't forget **to get wet to stay cool**. / … **to stay cool by getting wet**.
- h The National Park would prefer people not **to hike / to walk to the river and back in one day**.

93

English word	In German
quietly	leise
well-known	bekannt
undiscovered	unentdeckt
enjoyable	angenehm
periodically	regelmäßig
dislike	nicht mögen
uphill	bergauf
dramatic	dramatisch
infrequently	selten

94 Today the Grand Canyon is a very **well-known** place but it was **undiscovered** for a very long time. **Periodically** there are thunderstorms which can be very **dramatic** over the canyon. Most animals **dislike** people but if you walk **quietly** along the paths in the National Park you will probably see a lot of them. Tourists find it very **enjoyable** to take photos of the deer and the other wildlife that they meet. There are snakes and mountain lions, too, but these are **infrequently** seen.

What is also nice about the Grand Canyon National Park is that most paths there are very flat so you seldom have difficult **uphill** walks to make unless you go to the bottom of the canyon.

95 Hi Chelsea,
We have been visiting the Grand Canyon National Park. At the entrance to it there is a big sign. We drove into the National Park and we found our hotel. The hotel was made out of wood and it looked like a very big garden hut. The next day we decided to go for a walk. There were lots of walks there so we took the one to Hermits Rest. It was a very flat path; you could also cycle on it but we didn't have any bikes. When we got to Hermits Rest there was a fantastic view. Some people walked a little way down the hill but we didn't. The Grand Canyon is a really super place to visit.
Have a nice day, (your first name)

96 *Frau:* Entschuldigung, kannst du mir helfen? Ich habe ein Schild über Berglöwen gesehen. Gibt es hier wirklich welche? Ist die Wahrscheinlichkeit groß, dass mir einer über den Weg läuft?

Du: **Ja, hier gibt es Berglöwen, aber nur am South Rim, und sie sind selten.**

Frau: Die Tiere sind doch bestimmt gefährlich. Warum verjagen die Ranger sie nicht?

Du: **Weil sie wollen, dass sowohl Menschen als auch Tiere den Nationalpark genießen.**

Frau: Ich wollte heute spazieren gehen. Gibt es dafür Ratschläge?

Du: **Ja. Sie sollten nicht alleine spazieren gehen. Schließen Sie sich am besten einer Gruppe an. Beim Wandern sollten Sie möglichst viel Lärm machen, um die Tiere zu verscheuchen. Falls Sie Kinder dabei haben, dürfen sie nicht weit vor oder hinter ihnen laufen und Sie müssen sie immer im Blick haben. Sie dürfen auch keine Lebensmittel liegen lassen.**

Frau: Aber wie soll ich mich verhalten, wenn ich dennoch auf einen Berglöwen treffe?

Du: **Laufen Sie nie weg. Gehen Sie stattdessen langsam rückwärts. Machen Sie sich groß, zum Beispiel, indem Sie die Arme über ihren Kopf strecken, und machen Sie viel Lärm. Bleiben Sie immer bei Ihrer Gruppe.**

Frau: Sollte ich irgendetwas machen, nachdem ich einen Berglöwen gesehen habe?

Du: **Ja. Sie sollten es einem Ranger erzählen.**

Frau: Warum?

Du: **Weil es hier sehr wenige Berglöwen gibt.**

Frau: Vielen Dank für deine Hilfe.

97
- **a** I forgot **to buy** Jane a birthday card. She will **be** angry with me.
- **b** Rob is afraid of **standing** on a snake. I would prefer not **to meet** one, either.
- **c** I hated **swimming/to swim** as a child.
- **d** **Travelling** in cars **makes** me tired.
- **e** Nina **walked** quietly through the forest yesterday.
- **f** I would like **to own** a fast car.
- **g** **Fishing** isn't a sport I like.
- **h** How about **staying** with us tonight?
- **i** I want **to read** instead of **watching** TV.
- **j** We **have just returned** from the national park. We **had** a great time there.
- **k** After **closing** the door, she **lost** her key.
- **l** It will be no use **phoning** Eva tonight, she **is flying** to America.
- **m** Harry **spoke** to Jane before he **went** on holiday.
- **n** I fancy **buying** some new clothes tomorrow.
- **o** We **talked** together a lot while **jogging**.

Topic 12: Need something done?

98
- **a** ComputerDoc
- **b** Sam's Garage
- **c** Rosie's Interiors
- **d** 0456/44228
- **e** Castle Beauty Centre
- **f** ComputerDoc's/ComputerDoc
- **g** www.cbc.com
- **h** Rosie's Interiors
- **i** ComputerDoc
- **j** Sam's Garage

99
- **a** Jane is having her car sprayed/painted./ Jane has her car sprayed/painted.
- **b** Harry is having his long hair cut./Harry has his long hair cut.
- **c** Tom is having his computer repaired./Tom has his computer repaired.
- **d** Mrs Flower is having new curtains fitted./Mrs Flower has new curtains fitted.
- **e** I am having my carpet cleaned./I have my carpet cleaned.
- **f** They are having their sofa changed./They have their sofa changed.

100 **a** Anne is having her coat repaired.

- [x] Someone is repairing the coat for Anne.
- [ ] Anne is repairing her coat herself.

b Trevor has driven to Newcastle.

- [ ] Someone has driven Trevor to Newcastle.
- [x] Trevor drove to Newcastle himself.

c Ronnie has sent an e-mail.

- [ ] Someone has sent Ronnie an e-mail.
- [x] Ronnie has sent the e-mail himself.

d Kathy has an e-mail sent.

- [x] Someone sent the e-mail for Kathy.
- [ ] Kathy sent the e-mail herself.

e We have our hotel room cleaned.

- [x] Someone is cleaning the hotel room.
- [ ] We cleaned the hotel room ourselves.

f They have taken some photos.

- [ ] Someone has taken the photos of the other people.
- [x] The people have taken the photos themselves.

g The tourists have had maps given.

- [x] Someone has given the tourists the maps.
- [ ] The tourists have bought the maps themselves.

h Michael has bought a map.

- [ ] Someone has bought a map for Michael.
- [x] Michael bought the map himself.

i The man had his garden hut built.

- [x] Someone built the garden hut for the man.
- [ ] The man had built the garden hut alone.

j The woman has designed the logo.

- [ ] Someone has designed the logo for the woman.
- [x] The woman has designed the logo herself.

102 *(example answer)*

Hello. My name is John Smith and I saw your advert in the newspaper. I have a problem with my computer – I think it has got a virus and I would like to know whether you can come to my house and solve the problem. My phone number is 0673/78345. Can you phone me today between 5 p.m.–9 p.m.? Thank you.

103 *Luke:* Hello Marie. Can you tell Anna that I can't meet her tonight. I'm having my car repaired.

Marie: That's no problem. Anna, **Luke kann dich heute Abend nicht treffen. Er lässt sein Auto reparieren**.

Anna: Oje! Was lässt er machen?

Marie: Ich frage ihn. Luke, **what are you having done to your car?**

Luke: I'm having a new door put in. Someone has damaged one of them and I can't close it.

Marie: Er sagt, dass **er eine neue Tür einbauen lässt. Jemand hat eine Tür beschädigt und er kann sie nicht schließen.**

104
- **a** Linda is having her photo taken.
- **b** Tony is having his eyes tested.
- **c** The girls are having their nails painted.
- **d** Sam had his bike repaired.
- **e** You can have your hair cut at "Hair&Style".
- **f** My parents had their living room decorated.
- **g** They will have their shoes made.
- **h** Sheila and Bruce have their dogs looked after when they go out.
- **i** They have their meal cooked (... for them).

Topic 13: Drop, cover, hold on

105

		true	false	not in the text
a	The advice is for everyone living in earthquake areas.	☐	☑	☐
b	The worst earthquake was more than 100 years ago.	☐	☐	☑
c	Tourists usually don't know what to do in an earthquake.	☑	☐	☐
d	Buildings in California shouldn't be badly damaged by an earthquake.	☑	☐	☐
e	If the earthquake doesn't stop quickly, find some shelter.	☐	☑	☐
f	You should lie down on the floor during the earthquake.	☐	☑	☐
g	If you are outside, stay far away from buildings.	☐	☐	☑
h	It is a good idea to be next to an outside wall.	☐	☑	☐
i	The police and firemen will look for people after an earthquake.	☐	☐	☑
j	When the earthquake has stopped, the danger has gone.	☐	☑	☐

106

- **a** The advice is only for people in California.
- **e** In the first few seconds of an earthquake you should crawl to find shelter.
- **f** You either find shelter or you sit near an inside wall or next to low furniture, curl up into a ball and put your hands over your head and neck.
- **h** What you mustn't do in an earthquake is stay near outside walls.
- **j** After an earthquake there is a lot of danger. The electricity may not work, therefore it could be dark, there could be water on the floor, damaged stairs and many other dangers.

107

☐

☐

☑

☐

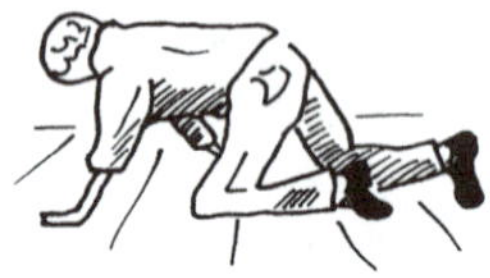

☑

☐

☐

☑

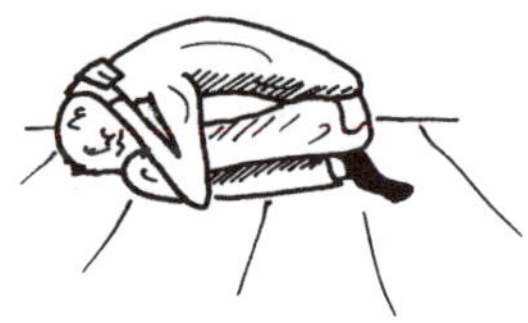

☑

108 a It wasn't raining, so the boys **could have played** football outside.
b Julie **could have flown / would have flown** if she had more money.
c I **could have caught / should have caught** an earlier bus but I didn't.
d Tom doesn't think he **should have eaten** so much at lunchtime – he's got stomach ache now.
e Sally **could have become** a doctor but she wanted to be a teacher.
f The girls **could have gone / should have gone** to the cinema but they went to the theatre instead.
g We **should have looked** at the weather forecast before we went to the beach – it rained!
h They **would have taken / should have taken** sandwiches with them but they didn't have enough bread.

109 a These four words **could have saved** many lives in the past.
b Anybody living in California **should have read** about what to do in an earthquake.
c But most visitors **wouldn't have thought** about earthquakes before they arrive.
d Many people **would have found** shelter under tables but there weren't any in the room.
e The man went under the table but he **should have held on** to it.
f The people who were hurt **shouldn't have sat** next to the outside wall.

110 a

verb	noun
(to) injure	**injury**
(to) protect	protection
(to) rescue	rescue
(to) shelter	**shelter**
(to) survive	survival
(to) warn	**warning**

b protector/rescuer/survivor

111 *(example poster)*

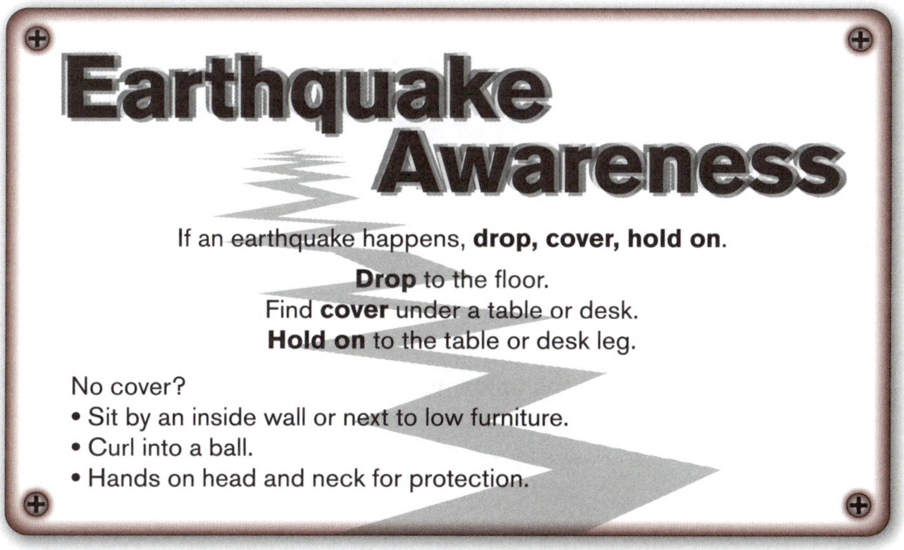

112
- a We **shouldn't have stayed** in Los Angeles; it wasn't very nice.
- b Rebecca **could have ridden** her bike faster but she didn't.
- c The lorry driver **couldn't have driven** over the bridge – it was too small for it.
- d The pilot **could have landed / should have landed** the plane in London but he flew on to Manchester.
- e They **wouldn't have gone / couldn't have gone** to the concert but their parents paid for it so they could.
- f The film **could have been / should have been** better than the book but it wasn't.

g I **should have visited** Jane when I was in London. She will be angry with me because I didn't.

h Tom **could have made/should have made** curry for his guests but he gave them fish and chips instead.

i You **should have walked** to school; it was quicker than the bus today.

j Sheila **would have phoned/should have phoned** me yesterday but she had to go to the doctor's.

k He **shouldn't have gone/couldn't have gone** to school yesterday; he had a very bad cold.

l Without Mike's help, we **couldn't have finished/wouldn't have finished** our work.

m It's too late now but I think we **should have bought** a bigger car.

Topic 14: The Glastonbury Festival

113 **a** They thought they were noisy, and the young people there drank too much and they took drugs.

b farmer: **Michael Eavis**
farm: **Worthy Farm**
village: **Pilton**

c ☑ true
☐ false

Why: The text says that the following year a second free festival was held. This means that there was a first free festival, too.

d There wasn't a Glastonbury Festival between 1971 and 1979.

e The village people …

☐ have complained about every festival since they started.
☑ soon saw that the festival had advantages for them.
☐ try to stop the festival every five years.

f music (concerts)/art events/selling clothes /clothes stalls/exhibitions (about green living)

g The type of artists who now comes to the festival are the superstars of the music world/famous singers and bands.

h It is difficult to get a ticket for the festival because they are quickly sold out.

i Farmers let their land rest every five years, the festival organisers do the same so every five years there isn't a festival.

114

Heading	Paragraph
The farmer and his festival	B
Badly organised	
Hugely successful	D
A quiet year	E
The weather	
Festival origins	A
Everyone is happy	C

115

a The people going to Woodstock were hippies.
b Many people complaining about the festival were old.
c The man organising the first Glastonbury Festival was a farmer.
d The free festivals held at Worthy Farm were the first two.
e The people living in Pilton like the festival.
f The bands playing today are usually very famous ones.
g The ticket found at the entrance was mine.
h The people helping at Glastonbury are volunteers.
i The money taken at the festival is usually used for a good project.
j The number of visitors coming to Glastonbury has increased.
k The people working at the festival are often students.
l The exhibitions giving information about green products are very popular.
m The land used at Worthy Farm needs a rest every five years.

116

"What do you think of the festival this year?"
"The band **playing** first weren't very good – and a bus **bringing** one band here was late."
"My grandparents gave me this photo. They are the two people **holding** the 'Peace' sign ... They still come with their hippie van. It's the one **broken down** in the field."
"Should we help them?"
"No, it happens every year. It's as old as they are. The tent **used** by them is also old ... When it rains, they get wet!"
"I can't believe the people **sleeping** in that tent are your grandparents!"

117

English word	explanation	German word
audience	the people who go to watch a pop festival, a film or a theatre show	*Publikum / Zuschauer*
busy	full – lots of people	*(hier) voll*
crowd	a lot of people	*(Menschen-)Menge / Zuschauermenge*
performer	the person who sings or dances, for example	*Künstler(in) / Musiker(in)*
rubbish	what is often left on the ground when everyone goes home – it should go into bins	*Müll*
security	the people or the situation which makes everyone safe at a big concert, for example	*Sicherheit*
stage	where the band play or actors act	*Bühne*
ticket	what you need to get into a concert, a film or a theatre, for example	*Eintrittskarte*

118 *(example answers)*

a The audience loved the band.
b The concert was very busy.
c There was always a very large crowd near the stage.
d The performers were very young.
e At the end of the concert most people took their rubbish home.
f There was a lot of security at the concert but there were no problems.
g There were two stages at the music festival.
h The tickets to get into the concert were expensive.

119 **a**

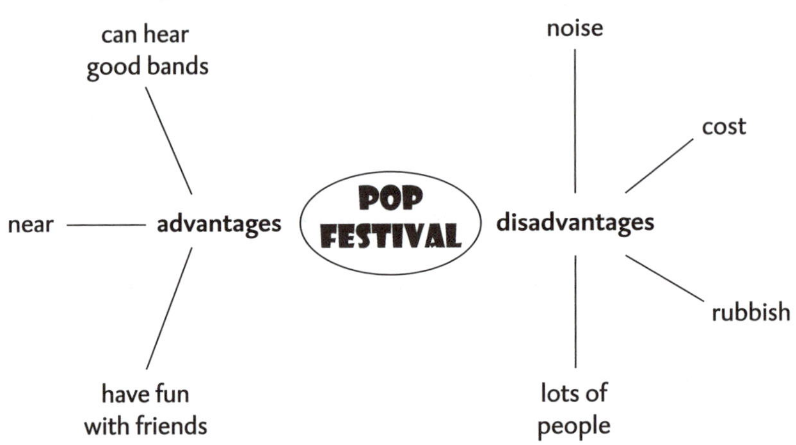

b *(example answer)*

An advantage of having a large pop festival in my home town is that I could walk to it. Of course the other advantages are that I could have fun with my friends since a lot of them could go, too. I really love music so if there was a pop festival, I could listen to some good bands playing live.
One disadvantage is that the tickets would be expensive. For people living in my town there would also be a lot of noise and a large number of people visiting the festival; I don't think many of them would like this. Finally, there could be a lot of rubbish which would need collecting. *(114 words)*

120
a The band playing first was not very good.
b A bus going to the concert broke down.
c The rubbish left after the concert has to be collected.
d The performers arriving this morning are well known.
e Judy's collapsed tent was old.
f The lost camera was Ian's./The camera lost at the festival was Ian's.
g The large crowd visiting the concert left quietly last night.
h The broken glasses were Charlie's.

Topic 15: Pier 39

121

	true	false	not in the text
a The Italians brought tourism with them. **This is false because the Italians started the fishing business here.**	☐	☑	☐
b There are not many fishermen left at the Wharf. **This is true because only some fishermen still go out in their boats.**	☑	☐	☐
c If you want to visit Alcatraz, you can from Fisherman's Wharf.	☐	☐	☑
d The sea lions came after an earthquake. **This is true because before the earthquake in 1989 there were no sea lions there.**	☑	☐	☐
e At first there were about 300 sea lions. **This is false because at first about 50 sea lions climbed onto the pontoons.**	☐	☑	☐

f	Something probably suddenly frightened the sea lions away. **This is false because when the fish left, they did too.**	☐	☑	☐
g	There are a lot of pontoons at Fisherman's Wharf.	☐	☐	☑
h	The sea lions are fun to watch. **This is true because tourists from all over the world watch them play.**	☑	☐	☐
i	A cleaner sea would help the sea lions. **This is true because rubbish in the sea is a big danger for them.**	☑	☐	☐

122 Pam **made** Jerry take her to Pier 39; he didn't really want to go. She wanted to throw the sea lions something to eat. Jerry said, "First, you **had better** ask someone if you can feed the sea lions."
Pam asked someone and, of course, the person at Pier 39 **didn't let** Pam feed them. That wasn't allowed, but he **let** her take lots of photos.
It was a very hot day and Jerry didn't like the sun. He told Pam that he **would rather** sit in the shade while she watched the sea lions. Jerry sat there for 30 minutes but then decided he **would rather** go shopping. Pam **made** Jerry leave most of his money with her because she didn't want him to spend a lot.

123
- **a** They **can fly/could fly** direct to America.
- **b** An hour ago, I **heard** Georgina **open** the door.
- **c** They don't like walking in the mountains, but they **do enjoy** walking on the beach.
- **d** Tony **saw** the car **stop** quickly.
- **e** My father was funny. He **would wear** a hat every day even when it was hot.
- **f** I **do believe/think** that you **should phone** Harry today.
- **g** We **heard** Gill **sing/singing** this morning.
- **h** **Can/Could** you **visit** Aunty Wendy in America, too?

124
- **a** ... one of San Francisco's **few** attractions ...
- **b** ... near the **beginning / start** of the 19th century ...
- **c** ... Fisherman's Wharf has **terrible / awful** restaurants ...
- **d** ... **bores** many people.
- **e** ... there were **a lot of / lots of / many** sea lions at Fisherman's Wharf ...
- **f** ... then **slowly** a few started to arrive ...
- **g** ... arrived in such **small** numbers ...
- **h** ... sea lions have now **left** Pier 39 ...
- **i** They **dislike / hate** routine ...

125 When we were in San Francisco, we went to Pier 39. It was a lovely hot day and lots of sea lions were already on the pontoons. The sea lions are very large and fun to watch. Three of them were on a pontoon very near to where I was. Two of the sea lions were barking at each other. They looked and sounded like they were having an argument. The third sea lion just slept while the other two were barking. I took a lot of photos of them before we left to look around Fisherman's Wharf. I wanted to stay longer but my sister said she would rather go shopping than watch the sea lions for hours. *(119 words)*

126
Mum: I think that we should **let** Robbie **plan** our holiday this year.
Janice: He **had better do** it well. I don't want a horrible one.
Robbie: We **could go** to California again. I enjoyed that last year.
Dad: I think Robbie's idea is super. We **could hire** a camper van.
Robbie: No, thanks. I **would rather stay** in hotels.
Janice: Me, too.
Dad: Okay. I **won't make** you **have** a holiday in one – it's just that I **do like** them. But, you **can look for** some nice hotels, Robbie.
Robbie: Okay, but where?
Mum: I **heard** someone **say** New England was nice. We **could go** there.
Janice: That's a great idea. **Let** us **do** that.

Stichwortverzeichnis

Englisch

Deutsch

Ihre Meinung ist uns wichtig!

Ihre Anregungen sind uns immer willkommen. Bitte informieren Sie uns mit diesem Schein über Ihre Verbesserungsvorschläge!

Titel-Nr.	Seite	Vorschlag

Lernen • Wissen • Zukunft
STARK

Bitte hier abtrennen

Zutreffendes bitte ankreuzen!

Die Absenderin/der Absender ist:

- ☐ Lehrer/in in den Klassenstufen: ______
- ☐ Fachbetreuer/in
  Fächer: ______
- ☐ Seminarlehrer/in
  Fächer: ______
- ☐ Regierungsfachberater/in
  Fächer: ______
- ☐ Oberstufenbetreuer/in
- ☐ Schulleiter/in
- ☐ Referendar/in, Termin 2. Staatsexamen: ______
- ☐ Leiter/in Lehrerbibliothek
- ☐ Leiter/in Schülerbibliothek
- ☐ Sekretariat
- ☐ Eltern
- ☐ Schüler/in, Klasse: ______
- ☐ Sonstiges: ______

Unterrichtsfächer: (Bei Lehrkräften!)

______

STARK Verlag
Postfach 1852
85318 Freising

21-V2X
Bitte ausfüllen und im frankierten Umschlag an uns einsenden. Für Fensterkuverts geeignet.

Kennen Sie Ihre Kundennummer?
Bitte hier eintragen.

Absender (Bitte in Druckbuchstaben!)

Name/Vorname

Straße/Nr.

PLZ/Ort/Ortsteil

Telefon privat

Geburtsjahr

E-Mail

Schule/Schulstempel (Bitte immer angeben!)

Bitte hier abtrennen

Sicher durch alle Klassen!

Faktenwissen und praxisgerechte Übungen mit vollständigen Lösungen.

Mathematik Realschule

Mathematik Grundwissen 5. Klasse .... Best.-Nr. 51405
Mathematik Grundwissen 5. Klasse Bayern .... Best.-Nr. 91410
Mathematik Grundwissen 5. Klasse Baden-W. ..... Best.-Nr. 81405
Mathematik Grundwissen 6. Klasse .... Best.-Nr. 51406
Mathematik Grundwissen 6. Klasse Bayern .... Best.-Nr. 914056
Mathematik Grundwissen 6. Klasse Baden-W. ..... Best.-Nr. 81406
Mathematik Grundwissen 7. Klasse .... Best.-Nr. 51407
Mathematik Grundwissen 7. Klasse Bayern .... Best.-Nr. 914057
Mathematik Grundwissen 7. Klasse Baden-W. .... Best.-Nr. 81407
Mathematik Grundwissen 8. Klasse Gruppe I und II/III Bayern .... Best.-Nr. 91406
Mathematik Grundwissen 8. Klasse Gruppe II/III Bayern .... Best.-Nr. 91419
Funktionen 8.–10. Klasse .... Best.-Nr. 91408
Übungsaufgaben Mathematik I 9. Klasse – Bayern .... Best.-Nr. 91405
Übungsaufgaben Mathematik II/III 9. Klasse – Bayern .... Best.-Nr. 91415
Mathematik Grundwissen 10. Kl. II/III Bayern ... Best.-Nr. 91417
Kompakt-Wissen Realschule Mathematik .... Best.-Nr. 914001

Deutsch Realschule

Deutsch Grundwissen 5. Klasse .... Best.-Nr. 91445
Deutsch Grundwissen 6. Klasse .... Best.-Nr. 91446
Deutsch Grundwissen 7. Klasse .... Best.-Nr. 91447
Deutsch Grundwissen 8. Klasse .... Best.-Nr. 91448
Rechtschreibung und Diktat 5./6. Kl. mit CD ...... Best.-Nr. 90408
Aufsatz 7./8. Klasse .... Best.-Nr. 91442
Erörterung und Textgebundener Aufsatz 9./10. Klasse .... Best.-Nr. 91441
Deutsch 9./10. Klasse Journalistische Texte lesen, auswerten, schreiben .... Best.-Nr. 81442
Übertritt in die Oberstufe .... Best.-Nr. 90409
Deutsch Rechtschreibung 5.–10. Klasse .... Best.-Nr. 934411
Kompakt-Wissen Deutsch Aufsatz .... Best.-Nr. 514401
Kompakt-Wissen Deutsch Aufsatz Bayern .... Best.-Nr. 914401
Kompakt-Wissen Rechtschreibung .... Best.-Nr. 944065

Englisch Realschule

Englisch Grundwissen 5. Klasse .... Best.-Nr. 91458
Englisch Grundwissen 6. Klasse .... Best.-Nr. 91459
Englisch Grundwissen 7. Klasse .... Best.-Nr. 914510
Englisch Grundwissen 8. Klasse .... Best.-Nr. 914511
Englisch Grundwissen 9. Klasse .... Best.-Nr. 914512
Englisch Grundwissen 10. Klasse .... Best.-Nr. 90510
Englisch Grundwissen 10. Klasse Baden-W. .... Best.-Nr. 81451
Englisch Übertritt in die Oberstufe .... Best.-Nr. 82453
Training Englisch Wortschatz – Mittelstufe .... Best.-Nr. 91455
Kompakt-Wissen Englisch Themenwortschatz ..... Best.-Nr. 914501
Kompakt-Wissen Englisch Grundwortschatz .... Best.-Nr. 914502
Sprachenzertifikat Englisch Niveau A 2 mit CD .... Best.-Nr. 105552
Sprachenzertifikat Englisch Niveau B 1 mit CD .... Best.-Nr. 105550

Geschichte/Sozialkunde

Kompakt-Wissen Realschule Geschichte .... Best.-Nr. 914801
Kompakt-Wissen Realschule Sozialkunde .... Best.-Nr. 914082

Französisch Realschule

Französisch im 1. Lernjahr .... Best.-Nr. 91462
Sprechfertigkeit 10. Klasse mit Audio-CD .... Best.-Nr. 91461
Rechtschreibung und Diktat 1./2. Lernjahr mit 2 CDs .... Best.-Nr. 905501
Wortschatzübung Mittelstufe .... Best.-Nr. 94510
Sprachenzertifikat DELF B1 mit MP3-CD .... Best.-Nr. 105530
Kompakt-Wissen Französisch Grundwortschatz ... Best.-Nr. 915001

Betriebswirtschaftslehre/Rechnungswesen

Betriebswirtschaftslehre/Rechnungswesen Grundwissen 8. Klasse Realschule Bayern .... Best.-Nr. 91473
Lösungsheft zu Best.-Nr. 91473 .... Best.-Nr. 91473L
Betriebswirtschaftslehre/Rechnungswesen Grundwissen 9. Klasse Realschule Bayern .... Best.-Nr. 91471
Lösungsheft zu Best.-Nr. 91471 .... Best.-Nr. 91471L
Betriebswirtschaftslehre/Rechnungswesen Grundwissen 10. Klasse Realschule Bayern .... Best.-Nr. 91472
Lösungsheft zu Best.-Nr. 91472 .... Best.-Nr. 91472L

VERA 8 Realschule

VERA 8 – Mathematik Version B: Realschule ...... Best.-Nr. 915082
VERA 8 – Deutsch mit MP3-CD Version B: Realschule .... Best.-Nr. 915482
VERA 8 – Englisch mit Audio-CD Version B: Realschule .... Best.-Nr. 915582

Klassenarbeiten/Schulaufgaben Realschule

Klassenarbeiten Mathematik 5. Klasse .... Best.-Nr. 510005
Schulaufgaben Mathematik 5. Klasse Bayern ..... Best.-Nr. 910001
Schulaufgaben Mathematik 6. Klasse Bayern ..... Best.-Nr. 910002
Schulaufgaben Mathematik 7. Klasse Gruppe I Bayern .... Best.-Nr. 910003
Schulaufgaben Mathematik 7. Klasse Gruppe II/III Bayern .... Best.-Nr. 910004
Schulaufgaben Mathematik 8. Klasse Gruppe II/III Bayern .... Best.-Nr. 910006
Schulaufgaben Mathematik 9. Klasse Gruppe I Bayern .... Best.-Nr. 910007
Schulaufgaben Mathematik 9. Klasse Gruppe II/III Bayern .... Best.-Nr. 910008
Klassenarbeiten Mathematik 10. Klasse .... Best.-Nr. 510010
Klassenarbeiten Deutsch 5. Klasse .... Best.-Nr. 1014051
Klassenarbeiten Deutsch 7. Klasse .... Best.-Nr. 1014071
Klassenarbeiten Englisch 6. Klasse .... Best.-Nr. 1015561
Klassenarbeiten Englisch 9. Klasse .... Best.-Nr. 1015591
Klassenarbeiten Französisch 9. Kl. mit MP3-CD ... Best.-Nr. 1015301

(Bitte blättern Sie um)